336 Ten-Minute Quilt Blocks

To Foundation-Piece, Quick-Piece, NoSew Appliqué, Stamp, Stencil, Paint & Embellish

by Holly L. Schmidt

Sterling Publishing Co., Inc. New York

A Sterling/Chapelle Book

We would like to offer our sincere appreciation of the valuable support given in this ever-changing industry of new ideas, concepts, designs, and products. Several projects shown in this publication were created with the outstanding and innovative products developed by:

Deco Art Americana Paints • P.O. Box 386; Stanford, KY 40484 • (606) 365-3193
Delta Technical Coatings • 2550 Pellissier Place; Whittier, CA 90601 • At arts and crafts stores nationwide
Duncan Enterprises; Aleene's Paints
Fiskars Scissors • P.O. Box 8027; Wausau, WI 54402-2091 • (715) 842-2091
Plaid Enterprises Inc. • P.O. Box 7600; Norcross, GA 30091-7600 • (800) 842-4197
Shirt Happens; Pic Shirt Photo Crafts; Photo Transfers • 1-800-952-4314

Library of Congress Cataloging-in-Publication Data

Schmidt, Holly L.
    336 ten-minute quilt blocks : to foundation-piece, quick-piece, NoSew appliqué, stamp, stencil, paint & embellish / Holly L. Schmidt.
        p.   cm.
    Includes index.
    ISBN 0-8069-1779-2
    1. Appliqué--Patterns. 2. Patchwork--patterns. 3. Wall hangings.
    4. Miniature quilts. 5. Fusible materials in sewing. I. Title.
TT779.S36 1998
746.46'041--dc21   98-34947
                                                CIP

10 9 8 7 6 5 4 3 2

A Sterling/Chapelle Book

First paperback edition published in 2000 by
Sterling Publishing Company, Inc.
387 Park Avenue South, New York, N.Y. 10016
Produced by Chapelle Ltd.
P.O. Box 9252, Newgate Station, Ogden, Utah 84409
© 1999 by Chapelle Limited
Distributed in Canada by Sterling Publishing
℅ Canadian Manda Group, One Atlantic Avenue, Suite 105
Toronto, Ontario, Canada M6K 3E7
Distributed in Great Britain and Europe by Cassell PLC
Wellington House, 125 Strand, London WC2R 0BB, England
Distributed in Australia by Capricorn Link (Australia) Pty Ltd.
P.O. Box 6651, Baulkham Hills, Business Centre, NSW 2153, Australia

Printed in China
All rights reserved

Sterling ISBN 0-8069-1779-2 Trade
            0-8069-2259-1 Paper

For Chapelle Limited
Owner: Jo Packham
Editor: Ann Bear
Staff: Marie Barber, Areta Bingham, Kass Burchett,
    Rebecca Christensen, Holly Fuller, Marilyn Goff,
    Shirley Heslop, Holly Hollingsworth,
    Sherry Hoppe, Shawn Hsu, Susan Jorgensen,
    Pauline Locke, Barbara Milburn, Linda Orton,
    Karmen Quinney, Leslie Ridenour, Cindy Stoeckl
Photography: Kevin Dilley, Photographer for Hazen
    Photography
Photo Stylist: Peggy Bowers

If you have any questions or comments, please contact:

        Chapelle, Ltd., Inc.
        P.O. Box 9252
        Ogden, UT 84409
        (801) 621-2777
        (801) 621-2788 Fax
        chapelle1@aol.com

Contents

336 Ten–Minute Quilt Blocks is designed with the beginning quilter in mind. Traditional quilting techniques, such as appliqué and piecing, have been adapted to make them easy, fast, and fun to do. For example, a quilt block that looks like it has been pieced is actually adapted from a quick iron–on appliqué technique. All of these quilt blocks, regardless of technique, were designed to be completed in ten minutes. The time it takes to make one quilt block may vary, depending on the quilter's own abilities.

With the exception of the foundation–pieced chapter, these quilt blocks are not designed for traditional quilts, to be extensively handled or worn, and were not meant to be laundered. These designs are offered as alternative ideas for wall hangings, mini quilts, Christmas stockings, table runners, and other decorative projects. However, if you choose, any of these original designs may be used in conjunction with traditional techniques to make such projects as quilts, clothing, and bags.

A Mini Gallery of project ideas for these quilt blocks is provided on pages 15–19. It may be used as a starting point for any ideas you may have while applying the easy techniques shown in this book.

The colorful borders on the edges of each page are designed to complement each set of quilt blocks and may be used as fabric borders in your quilt or project. Although there are no accompanying patterns, the borders themselves may be copied and used as patterns. Instructions for quilt block assembly also apply to border assembly.

Instructions and additional options, which apply to all the quilt blocks for an individual theme, are provided in the left column of each page and are labeled "General" and "General Option." Instructions that apply to specific quilt blocks in the same theme are provided in the right column and are labeled "Specific" and "Specific Idea".

Patterns are provided alongside each quilt block. Each pattern piece has been colored a solid color. To use these patterns, the following example is provided. Leave extra fabric on the underside pieces, as indicated in the following diagrams. We recommend this method rather than trying to butt the fabric edges together. However, if you choose, you may butt fabric edges together.

Block as shown on page 73.

General Option: Use Plastic "googly eyes".

Pattern as shown on page 73.

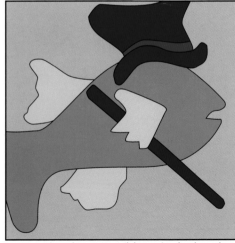

Specific Idea: Use ribbon for hatband.

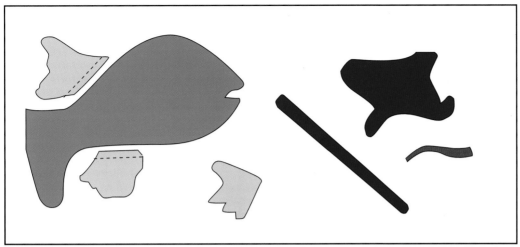

Diagram 1

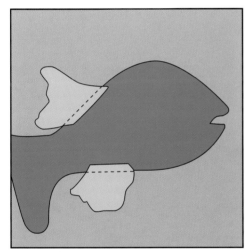

Diagram 2

1. Trace and cut out each pattern piece, as shown in Diagram 1.

2. Place outer fin allowances under fish body. Fuse all pieces at one time for proper placement, as shown in Diagram 2.

3. Fuse hat and cane onto fish body, as shown in Diagram 3.

4. Fuse hat band onto hat and top fin onto cane, as shown in Diagram 4.

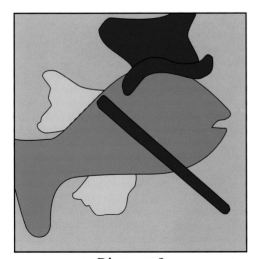

Diagram 3

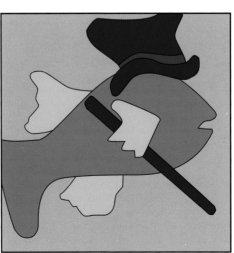

Diagram 4

Attaching Motifs

Most appliqué quilt blocks can take more than ten minutes to assemble. The NoSew appliqué blocks are fused together with either double–sided adhesive or fusible web. The option remains to appliqué the block, using traditional quilting techniques. Refer to a book on appliquéing for more detailed instructions on this technique.

Attaching Motifs with Double–sided Adhesive

1. Always pretest double–sided adhesive on fabric to be used.

2. Peel off paper backing.

3. Adhere sticky side onto wrong side of fabric.

4. Trace pattern onto paper backing, using a marking tool. Cut out pattern, following traced lines.

5. Adhere fabric motifs onto block, following manufacturer's instructions.

Attaching Motifs with Fusible Web

1. Trace pattern onto tracing paper, using a marking tool.

2. Turn tracing paper over so pattern is reversed.

3. Place fusible web, paper side up, on reversed pattern.

4. Trace pattern onto paper side of fusible web.

5. Cut out pattern on fusible web, leaving a ¼" border around pattern.

6. Fuse the fusible web onto the motif fabrics, following manufacturer's instructions.

7. Cut out motif, following pattern line.

8. Fuse the fabric motifs onto block.

Note: Throughout 336 Ten-Minute Quilt Blocks, details, such as eyes, flower stems, and "stitch lines", are drawn onto motifs, using fabric pens. Buttons, beads, and other embellishments are adhered onto motifs with fabric glue. The option remains to use more traditional quilting techniques rather than these time–saving techniques.

Batting

Batting is not intended to be used with most quilt blocks in this book. Batting is traditionally used as the middle layer of a quilt or sometimes in clothing and doll making. If 336 Ten–Minute Quilt Blocks patterns will be fashioned into finished projects requiring batting, please refer to a book on the traditional quilt technique that you will be using.

Bonded cotton batting gives a flat, natural appearance and comes in varying thicknesses. Polyester batting gives a puffy appearance. Felt may be substituted and renders the same appearance as bonded cotton batting.

Enlarging Patterns

All patterns shown are 2½" x 2½". Patterns may be enlarged or reduced, using a photocopy machine, if the finished block is to be larger or smaller than the pattern shown. It is best to use a professional copy shop. For a 4" x 4" block, enlarge 160%; for a 6" x 6" block, enlarge 240%; for a 8" x 8" block, enlarge 318%.

Fabric Paints & Pens

Painting on Fabric

Painting on fabric requires the use of purchased, premixed textile paints or, if colors desired are not available, the use of a textile medium. A textile medium is mixed with acrylic paint to make it glide over fabric and permeate the fibers. When using acrylic paints, add a few drops of textile medium to paint and mix well. The paint will become more transparent as more textile medium is added. Paint may be diluted with water. It prevents paint from bleeding and makes the painting, when dry, permanent.

Fabrics should be washed and then ironed. Stretch taut while painting, using embroidery hoops, to prevent bubbling or puckering. Use fabric paints, following manufacturer's instructions.

1. Trace pattern onto fabric, using marking tool. Cut out and assemble motifs, if applicable.

2. Paint fabric, following transferred pattern lines. Allow paint to dry thoroughly.

3. Heat–set fabric in a dryer or with a warm iron on the reverse side of the fabric.

Painting with Fabric Pens

Fabric pens can be used to apply permanent color to fabrics and do not need to be heat–set. Use fabric pens, following manufacturer's instructions.

1. Trace pattern onto fabric, using marking tool. Cut out and assemble motifs, if applicable.

2. Fill in transferred pattern with fabric pens. Blend colors to give design a softened, more realistic, or dimensional look.

3. Use a blender pen to mix two or more colors, or color one color over another until a different shade is achieved.

Fabrics & Threads

Fabrics need to be selected for backgrounds and individual motifs. The texture, color, and print of fabrics used will depend on the desired look of the finished project, as well as the skill of the crafter. Each fabric chosen should be appropriate for the use of the finished project—a piece that will be frequently laundered should not be made from nonwashable fabrics. Also, keep in mind how easily a particular fabric frays. A fabric that frays very easily will be hard to work with and the edges will have to be secured in some way. Raw edges can generally be cut with pinking shears to prevent fraying, or use a liquid fray preventive.

Quilting fabrics include calico, muslin, and broadcloth. They are medium–weight fabrics made from 100% cotton. Calico and other printed fabrics are available in a variety of patterns and colors. Muslin is white or off–white and is usually used for the background in a pieced design. Broadcloth is a plain–weave fabric and generally a solid color.

Before marking and/or cutting on fabrics, make certain fabrics have been laundered, dried, and pressed. This will preshrink fabrics. It is necessary to test fabric to make certain it is colorfast. Do not trust manufacturer's labels. Cut a 2"–wide strip of each fabric selected for quilt block, cutting crosswise. To determine whether fabrics are colorfast, place each strip separately into a clean bowl of extremely hot water, or hold each fabric strip under hot running water and place on white paper towel. If fabric bleeds, wash until all excess dye has been washed out. Fabrics which continue to bleed after washing several times should not be used.

The type of fabric chosen will affect the choice of thread used. Threads should go with like fabrics—natural threads with natural fabrics and synthetic threads with synthetic fabrics.

Embroidery threads of all kinds may be used. The color and character of embroidery thread usually coordinate with the fabric used, but not always. Sometimes contrasting stitching adds as much to the design as the fabric itself.

Foundation Piecing

Foundation Piecing

Foundation piecing is sewing fabric onto a foundation, following a numerical sequence. Sewing lines are drawn on the foundation. Fabric is placed on the unmarked (right) side while being sewn on the marked (wrong) side. Foundation piecing allows the quilter to piece even the tiniest pieces more quickly and accurately since all sewing will follow drawn lines.

Foundation Materials

Decide what type of foundation to use—fabric, paper, or tear–away interfacing. If using fabric, choose a light–colored, lightweight fabric that can be seen through for tracing; cotton and muslin work well. Be certain to test foundation and quilt fabrics for shrinkage. If using paper, choose one that can be seen through, such as notebook paper, copy paper, newsprint paper, or computer paper. This tears away after sewing is completed. If choosing tear–away interfacing, choose one that can be removed easily.

Mirror Images

Foundation piecing will create a mirror image of the pattern. If an exact replica of the pattern is desired, reverse the pattern on the foundation.

Step by Step for Foundation Piecing

1. Transfer pattern onto foundation. Using a fine–point permanent marking pen, write all numbers on foundation.

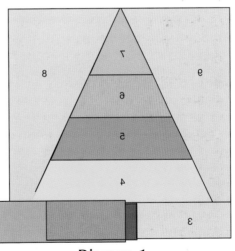

2. Turn over foundation with unmarked side up. Place fabric piece 1, right side up, on shape 1. Hold foundation up to a light source to make certain that fabric overlaps at least ¼" on all sides of shape 1. Pin or glue in place.

Diagram 1

3. Make certain that fabric piece 2 overlaps at least ¼" on all sides of shape 2. Place fabric piece 2 on fabric piece 1, right sides together as shown in Diagram 1.

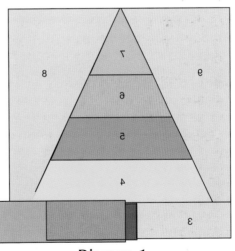

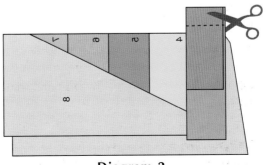

4. Turn over foundation with marked side up. Fold foundation along line between shapes 1 and 2. Trim both fabric pieces ¼" from fold line as shown in Diagram 2.

5. Sew along line between shapes 1 and 2 with marked side of foundation up,

Diagram 2

9

using a very small stitch (to allow for easier paper removal). Begin and end two or three stitches beyond line as shown in Diagram 3.

6. Turn over foundation with unmarked side up. Open fabric piece 2 and finger-press seam. Pin or adhere in place.

7. Turn over foundation with marked side up. Fold foundation along line between shapes 2 and 3. Trim fabric piece 2 to ¼" from fold. Unfold foundation.

8. Make certain that fabric piece 3 overlaps at least ¼" on all sides of shape 3. Place fabric piece 3 on fabric piece 2 with right sides together and even with trimmed edge of fabric piece 2 as shown in Diagram 4. Pin or adhere in place.

9. Turn over foundation with marked side up. Sew along line between shapes 2 and 3. Begin and end sewing two or three stitches beyond line.

10. Turn over foundation with unmarked side up. Open fabric piece 3, and finger-press seam. Pin or adhere in place.

11. Turn over foundation with marked side up. Fold foundation forward along line between shapes 1, 2, 3, and 4. If previous stitching makes it difficult to fold foundation, pull paper foundation away from fabric at stitching, then fold along line. If using a fabric foundation, fold it forward as far as it will go and trim to ¼" from drawn line as shown in Diagram 5.

12. Continue trimming and sewing fabric pieces in numerical order until block is complete. Press block, then trim fabric even with outside line of foundation to

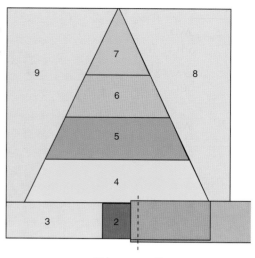

Diagram 3

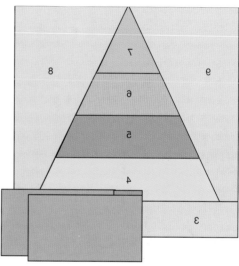

Diagram 4

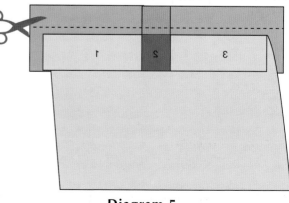

Diagram 5

complete block as shown in Diagram 6. If sewing blocks together, do not remove paper or tear away interfacing at this time. Since grain line was not considered and many edges may be stretchy, bias block the edges.

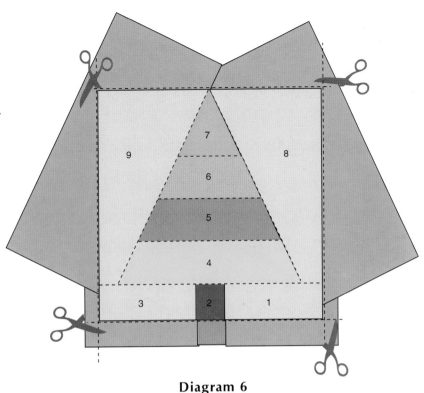

Diagram 6

Marking Tools

Test the marking tool on fabric first to make certain marks can be removed easily. Always use a light hand when marking with any marking tool. To mark around cardboard templates on light–colored fabrics, use a sharp #2 lead pencil. On dark–colored fabrics, use a sharp white dressmaker's pencil, a sliver of soap, or a yellow or silver fabric marking pencil. Chalk pencils or chalk–wheel markers make light marks on dark–colored fabrics. Disappearing ink pens may be used when marking light–colored fabrics. Fine–point permanent markers and transfer pens may be used for foundation piecing.

Pattern Tracing

Tracing onto Fabric

1. For lightweight fabrics, place fabric over pattern and trace with a marking tool.

2. Draw straight lines, including all numbers where applicable, using a ruler and a marking tool.

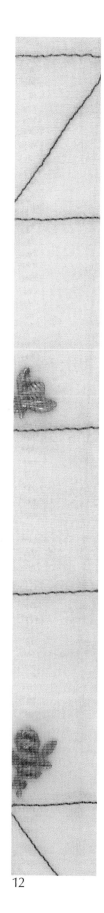

3. Draw a line ¼" around the outside edges of block, cut along outside drawn line. Repeat for number of blocks desired.

Using a Transfer Pen

Block patterns can be transferred to foundation from tracing paper, using a transfer pen. This technique will result in a mirror image of the pattern.

1. Trace pattern onto paper, using a transfer pen.

2. Iron transfer onto foundation fabric, following manufacturer's instructions.

3. Write all numbers where applicable, using a marking tool.

Photo Transfers

Two techniques can be used for transferring photos. Before beginning project, read instructions below, and decide which technique is preferred. Photo transfer medium and photo transfer paper may be found at local craft or fabric stores. When using these techniques, printed letters in photographs will need to be reversed when copying, or words will be mirrored.

Note: Results from either technique may vary depending on temperature and humidity.

Photo Transfer Medium

1. Take photograph to a copy shop and photocopy. Explain the exact look desired before the photocopy is made. Copy onto white copy paper.

2. Transfer copy of photograph to white or light–colored fabric, using photo transfer medium, following manufacturer's instructions.

Photo Transfer Paper

1. Take photograph and photo transfer paper to a copy shop and photocopy on photo transfer paper. Photo transfer paper will only pick up an image once. Any white space cannot be run through a copy machine again. Explain to the printer the exact look desired before the photocopy is made.

2. Place photo transfer paper on fabric with image to right side of fabric.

3. Press photo transfer paper to fabric, using a heated dry iron, until image has been successfully transferred. Remove paper backing from fabric, following manufacturer's instructions.

Note: After transfer is complete, never touch transfer with a hot iron. If ironing is necessary, you may place waxed paper or discarded web backing over transfer and iron on wrong side of fabric.

Piecing

Most pieced quilt blocks can take more than ten minutes to assemble. The quick–pieced blocks in this book are NoSew appliquéd, allowing for the look of a pieced quilt block without the time associated with piecing. The option remains to piece the block, using traditional quilting techniques. Refer to a book on piecing for more detailed instructions on this technique.

Rotary Cutters, Scissors & Pinking Shears

Rotary Cutters & Fabric Scissors are used for cutting fabric and should be designated for that purpose only. Using these tools to cut other materials will dull the blades and make them less effective.

Craft Scissors are essential for cutting cardboard, paper, and acetate templates. They are very strong and have a very refined cutting edge, which makes it possible to get in tight areas.

Embroidery Scissors are generally used only for cutting threads.

Pinking Shears have notched or serrated blades. They are used to cut edges of fabric with a zigzag pattern for decorative purposes and are often used to prevent edges of fabric from fraying.

Rubber Stamps

There are many inks and paints available for use with rubber stamps on fabric. Some inks and paints require heat–setting. Use inks and paints, following manufacturer's instructions.

Choose fabrics with care. Inks or paints needing to be heat–set will not work well on fabrics that should not be heated. Polished cottons, canvas, and tight–weave fabrics work well. Loose–weave, stretch–weave, furry, and nubby fabrics should not be used. If fabric will be worn, prewash to remove sizing. When prewashing, do not use a fabric softener. A fabric softener can coat fabric with a stain guard, preventing successful stamping. Test the stamp on a piece of fabric and wash to determine whether ink or paint will bleed, run, or fade with washing.

Place fabric on cardboard or stretch over a frame to make stamping on fabric easier.

Waxed paper can be ironed onto the back, or clear shelf paper adhesive can be used to keep fabric from stretching.

1. Stamp fabric with desired image.

2. Fill in stamped areas, using fabric pens or textile paint.

3. Heat–set if necessary.

S tencils

1. Make one copy of pattern for each color change, for example make three copies for the pattern below.

2. To make stencil, cut out portion of first shape from first copy, using a craft knife or single–edged razor. Using a piece of glass for a cutting surface will make cutting easier. Repeat for second and third shapes.

3. Tape stencil for lightest color on fabric with masking tape or stencil mask.

4. Color shape with stencil cream or paste.

5. Repeat steps 3 and 4 for each stencil, working from lightest to darkest color, taping over already colored shapes. Draw details, using fabric pens.

Pattern as shown on page 94.

Each color is a separate stencil.

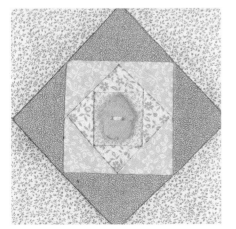

PHOTO ALBUM COVER

made with Family Photographs quilt blocks, pages 124–125.

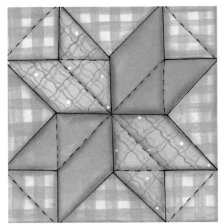

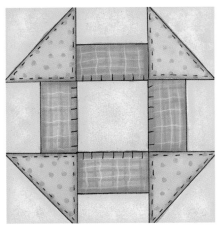

17

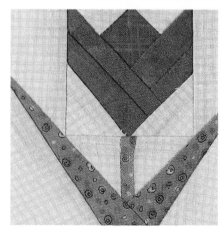

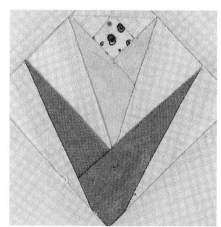

P LACE MAT

made with Vegetables quilt blocks, pages 94–95.

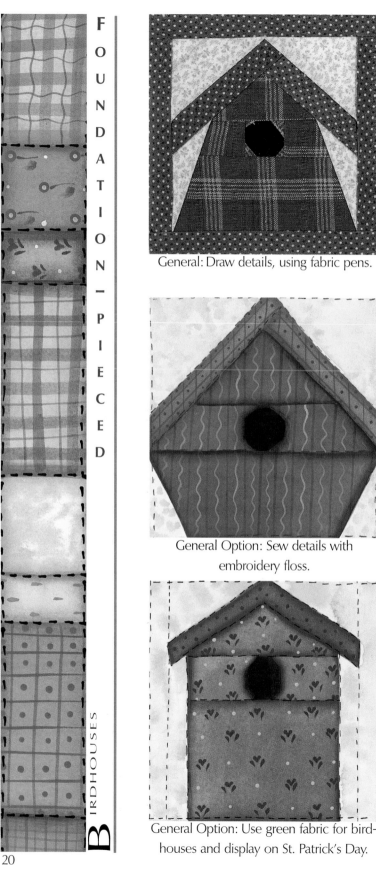

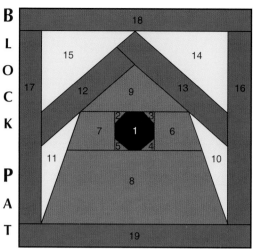

General: Draw details, using fabric pens.

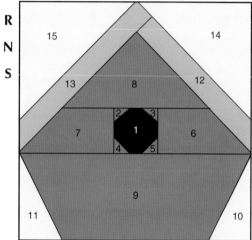

Specific Idea: Attach bird button to birdhouse roof.

General Option: Sew details with embroidery floss.

Specific Idea: Write "Home Tweet Home" on birdhouse, using fabric pens.

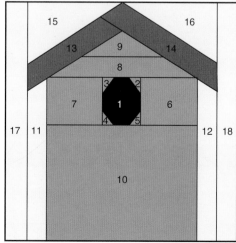

General Option: Use green fabric for birdhouses and display on St. Patrick's Day.

Specific Idea: Write "For Rent" on birdhouse, using fabric pens.

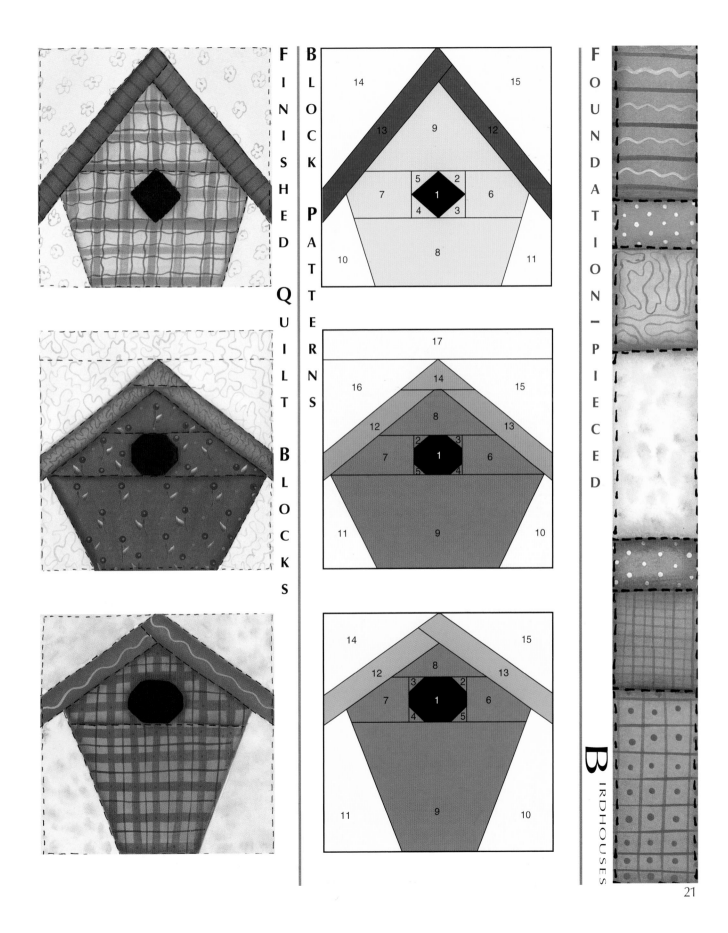

BLOCK PATTERNS

14

15

13

9

12

5   2
7   1   6
4   3

10

8

11

17

16   14   15

12   8   13

2   3
7   1   6
5   4

11   9   10

14

15

12   8   13

3   2
7   1   6
4   5

11   9   10

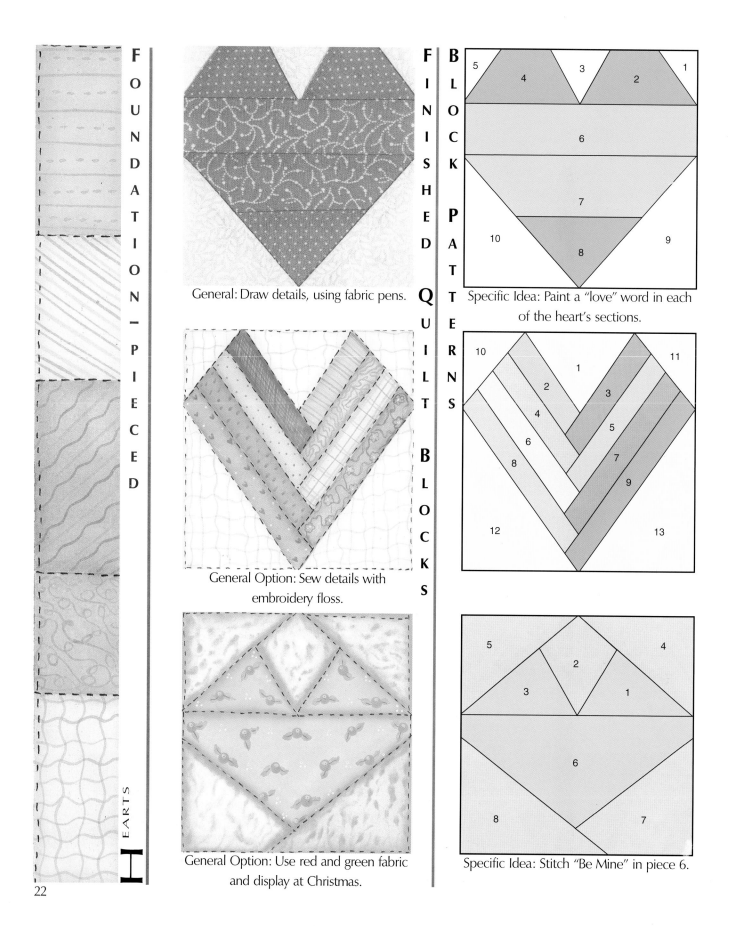

General: Draw details, using fabric pens.

General Option: Sew details with embroidery floss.

General Option: Use red and green fabric and display at Christmas.

F I N I S H E D   Q U I L T   B L O C K S

B L O C K   P A T T E R N S

5 4 3 2 1 6 7 10 8 9

Specific Idea: Paint a "love" word in each of the heart's sections.

10 1 2 3 4 5 6 7 8 9 11 12 13

5 2 4 3 1 6 8 7

Specific Idea: Stitch "Be Mine" in piece 6.

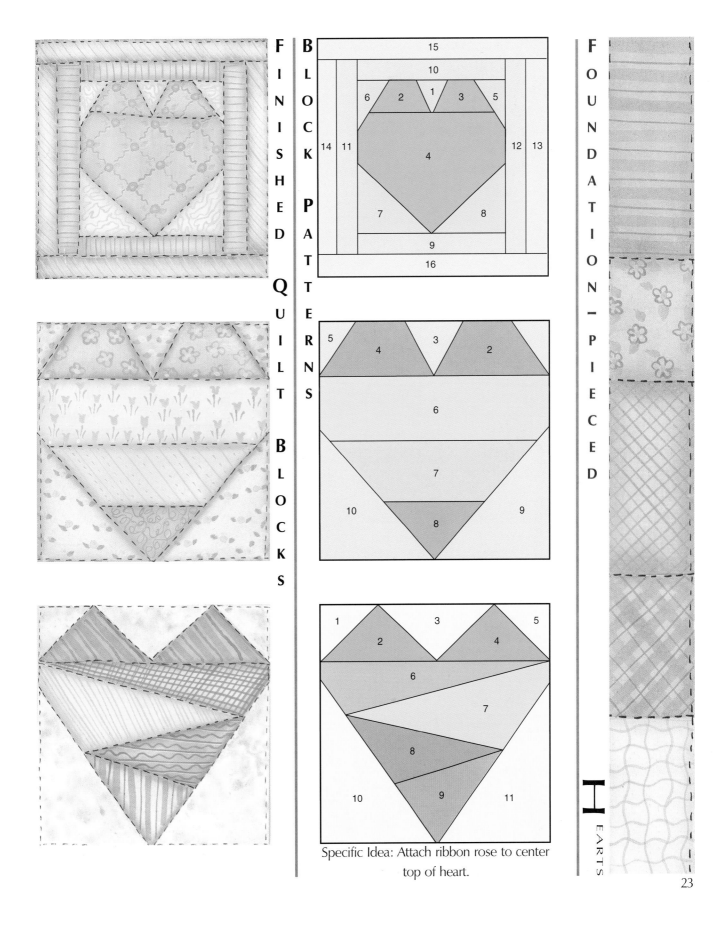

FINISHED QUILT BLOCKS

BLOCK PATTERNS

Block 1

| 15 |
| 10 |

6	2	1	3	5
14	11	4	12	13
7	8
9
16

Block 2

| 5 | 4 | 3 | 2 |
| 6 |
| 7 |
| 10 | 8 | 9 |

Block 3

| 1 | 3 | 5 |
| 2 | 4 |
| 6 |
| 7 |
| 8 |
| 10 | 9 | 11 |

Specific Idea: Attach ribbon rose to center top of heart.

FOUNDATION–PIECED

HEARTS

23

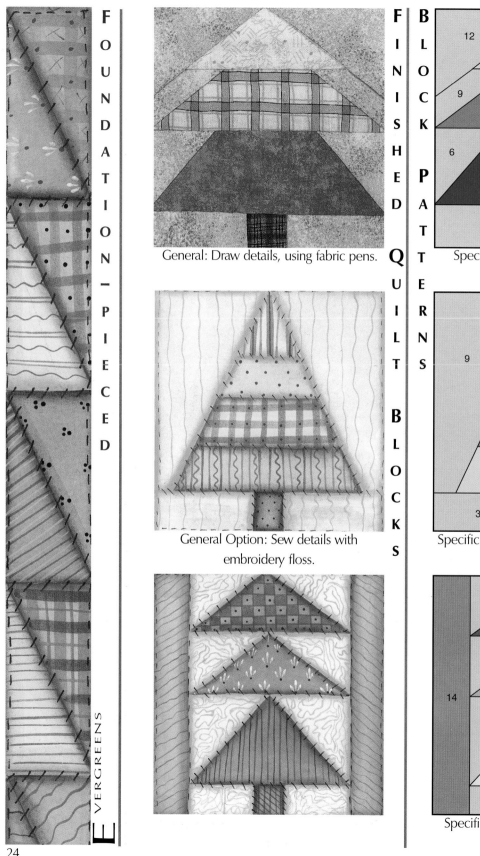

FOUNDATION–PIECED

EVERGREENS

FINISHED QUILT BLOCKS

BLOCK PATTERNS

General: Draw details, using fabric pens.

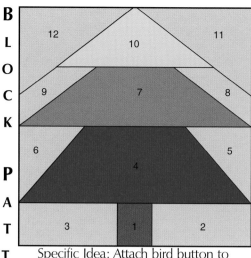

Specific Idea: Attach bird button to piece 7.

General Option: Sew details with embroidery floss.

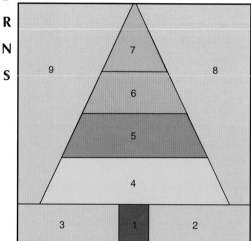

Specific Idea: Attach seed beads to tree's sections for ornaments.

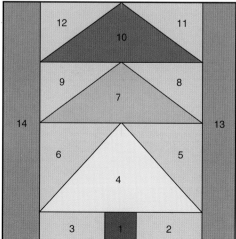

Specific Idea: Hang charms from tree's sections.

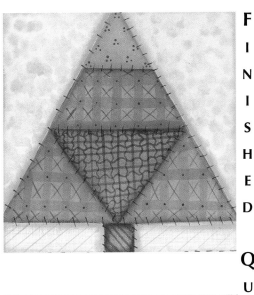

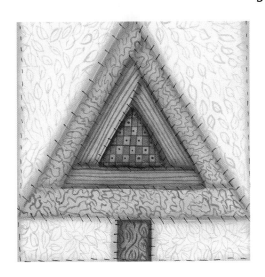

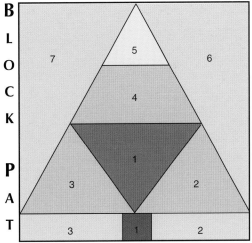

Specific: Sew top and bottom as separate pieces, then attach.

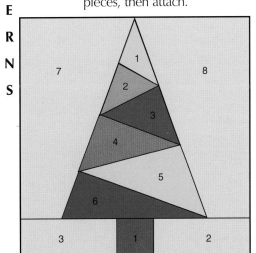

Specific: Sew top and bottom as separate pieces, then attach.

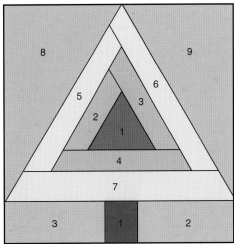

Specific: Sew top and bottom as separate pieces, then attach.

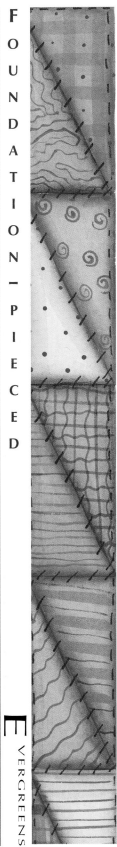

25

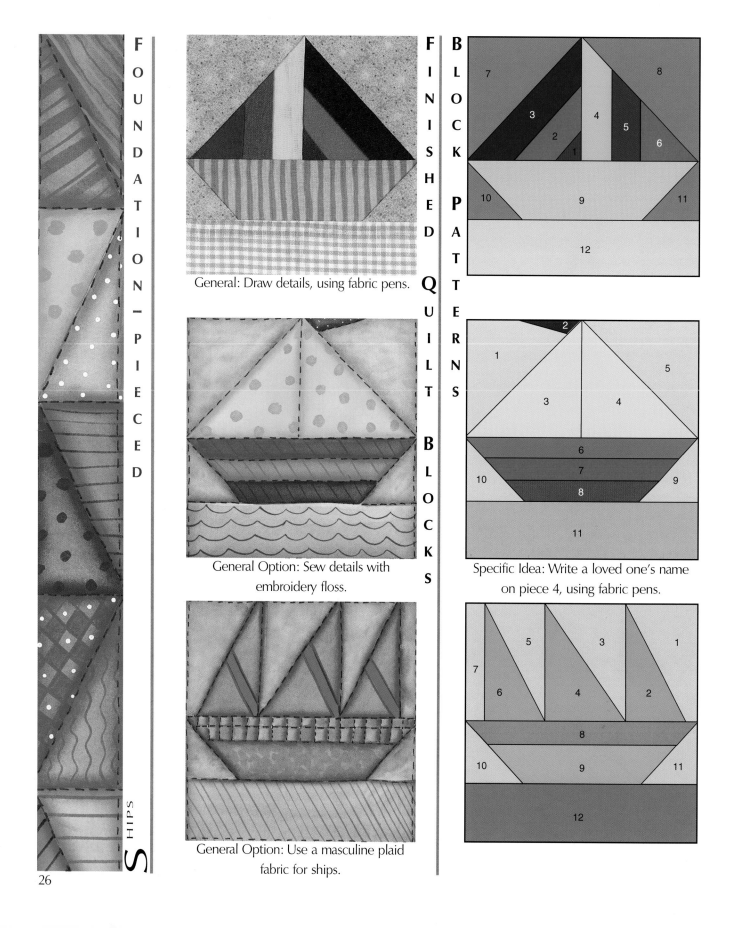

General: Draw details, using fabric pens.

General Option: Sew details with embroidery floss.

General Option: Use a masculine plaid fabric for ships.

Specific Idea: Write a loved one's name on piece 4, using fabric pens.

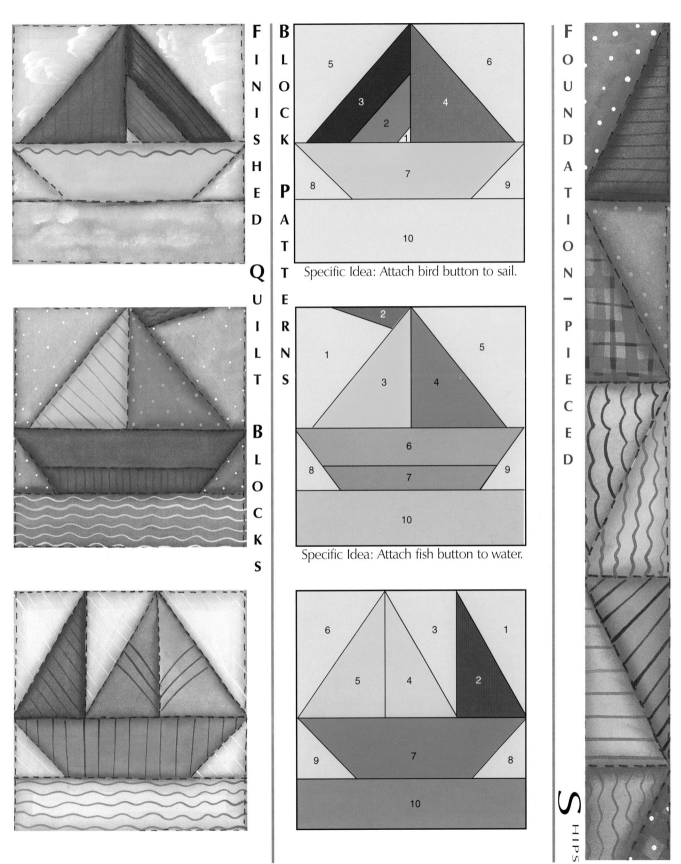

Specific Idea: Attach bird button to sail.

Specific Idea: Attach fish button to water.

SHIPS

General: Draw details, using fabric pens.

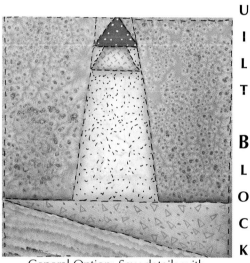

General Option: Sew details with embroidery floss.

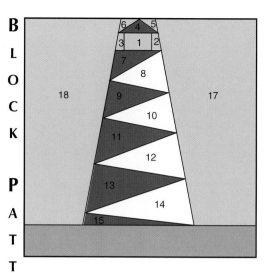

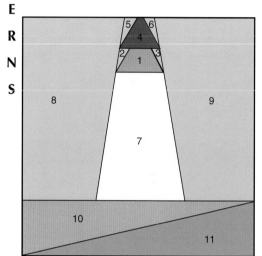

Specific Idea: Paint lighthouse light with metallic paint.

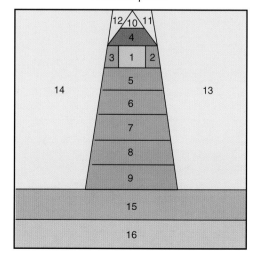

28

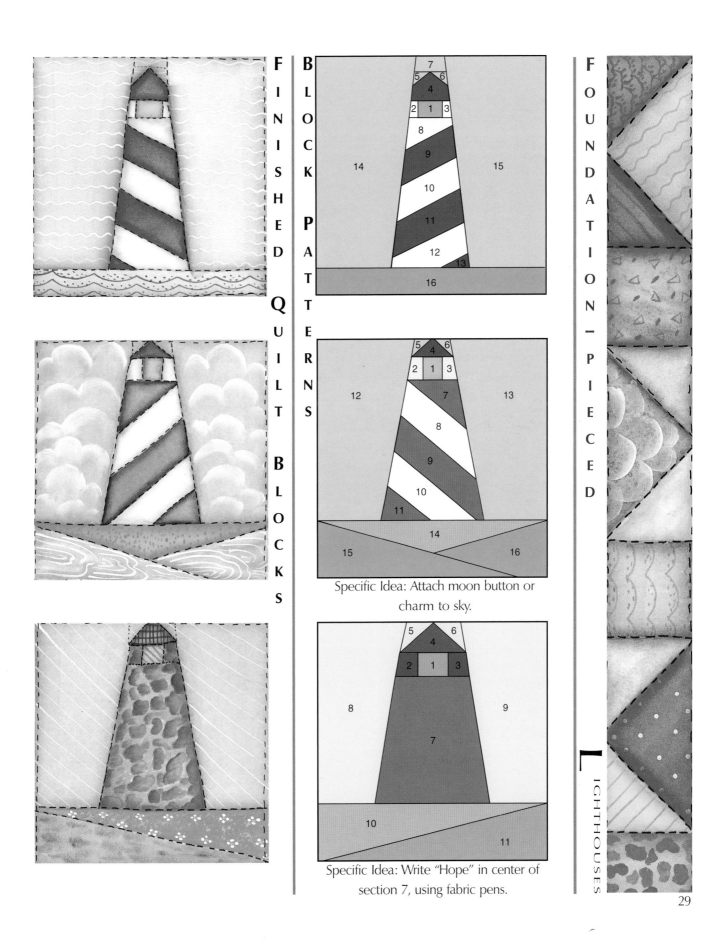

7
5 6
4
2 1 3
8
9
10
14
15
11
12
13
16

5 6
4
2 1 3
7
8
12
13
9
10
11
14
15
16

Specific Idea: Attach moon button or charm to sky.

5 6
4
2 1 3
8
9
7
10
11

Specific Idea: Write "Hope" in center of section 7, using fabric pens.

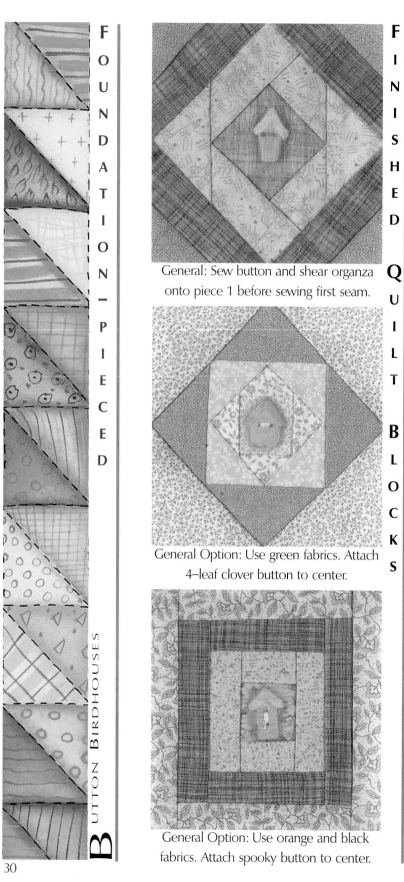

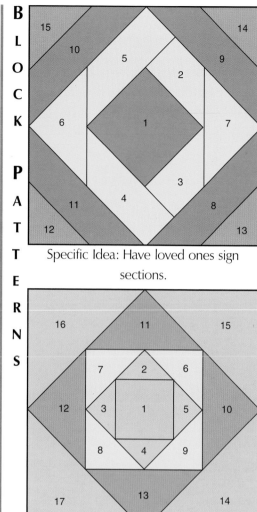

General: Sew button and shear organza onto piece 1 before sewing first seam.

General Option: Use green fabrics. Attach 4–leaf clover button to center.

General Option: Use orange and black fabrics. Attach spooky button to center.

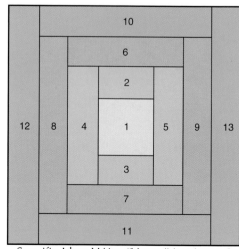

Specific Idea: Have loved ones sign sections.

Specific Idea: Write "Home" in pieces 6 and 7 and "Sweet" in pieces 8 and 9.

F I N I S H E D

Q U I L T

B L O C K S

B L O C K P A T T E R N S

F O U N D A T I O N – P I E C E D

B UTTON B IRDHOUSES

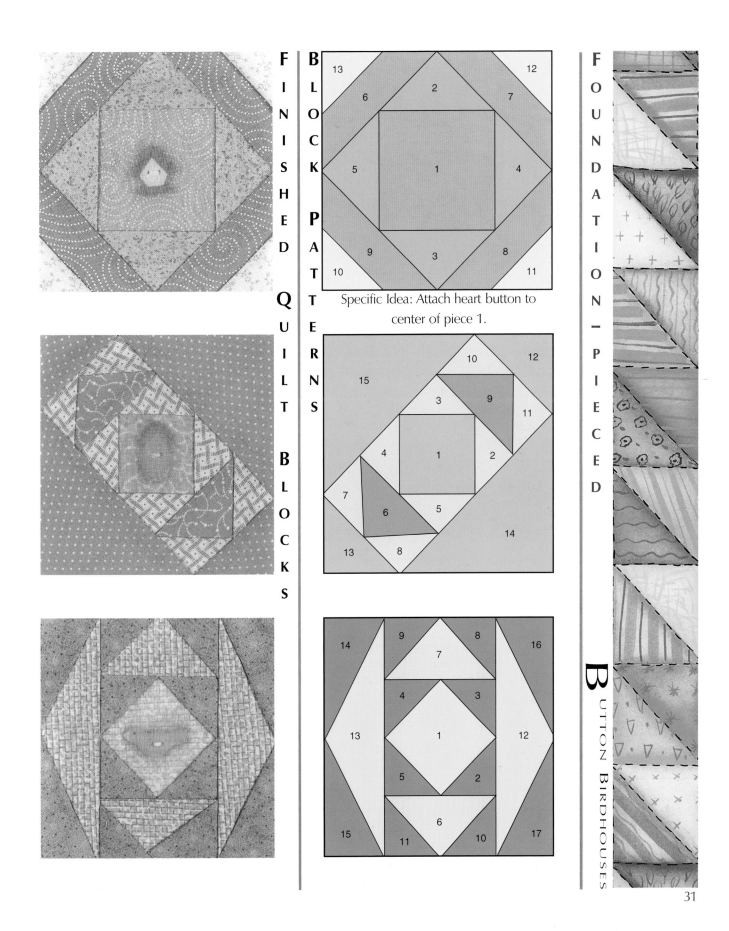

13		2		12
6			7	
5		1		4
	9	3	8	
10				11

Specific Idea: Attach heart button to center of piece 1.

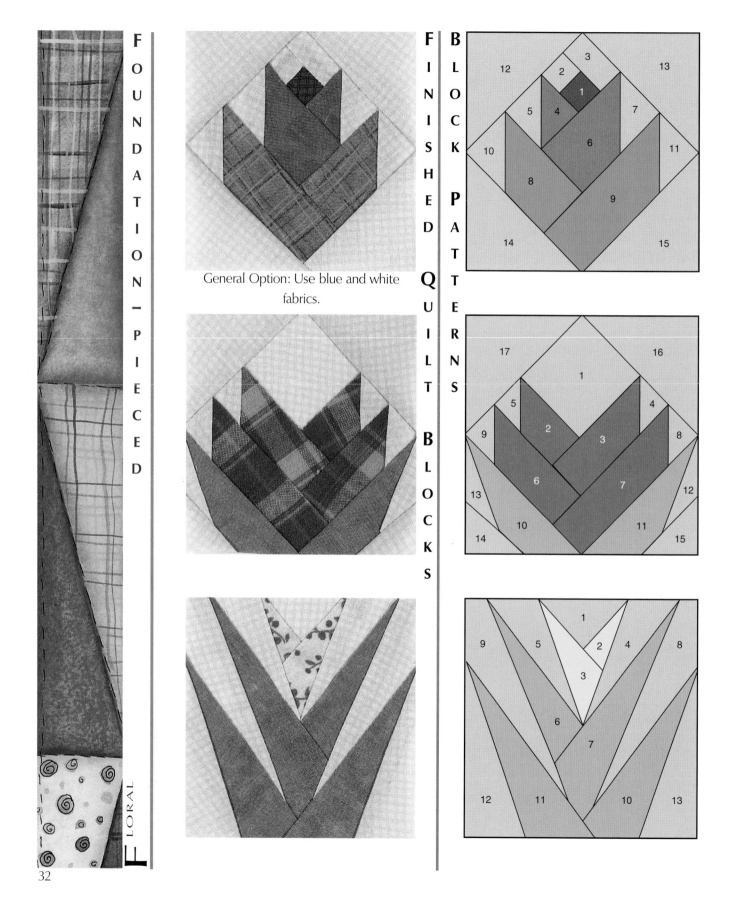

General Option: Use blue and white fabrics.

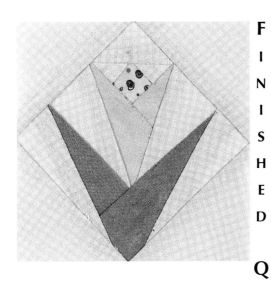

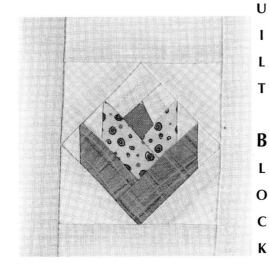

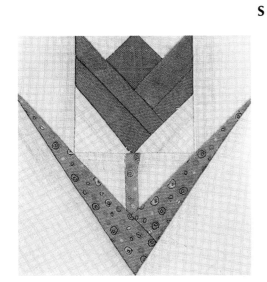

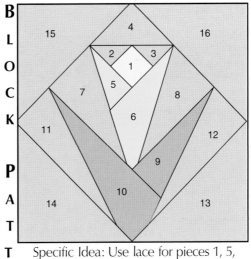

Specific Idea: Use lace for pieces 1, 5, and 6.

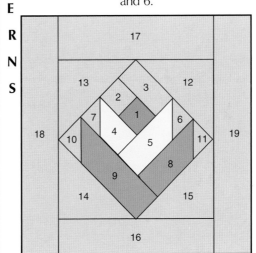

Specific Idea: Write "nature" words in pieces 16, 17, 18, and 19.

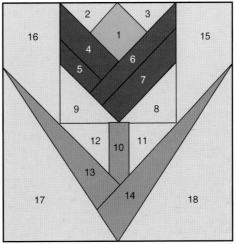

Specific Idea: Use red fabric for pieces 1, 4, 5, 6, and 7.

FLORAL

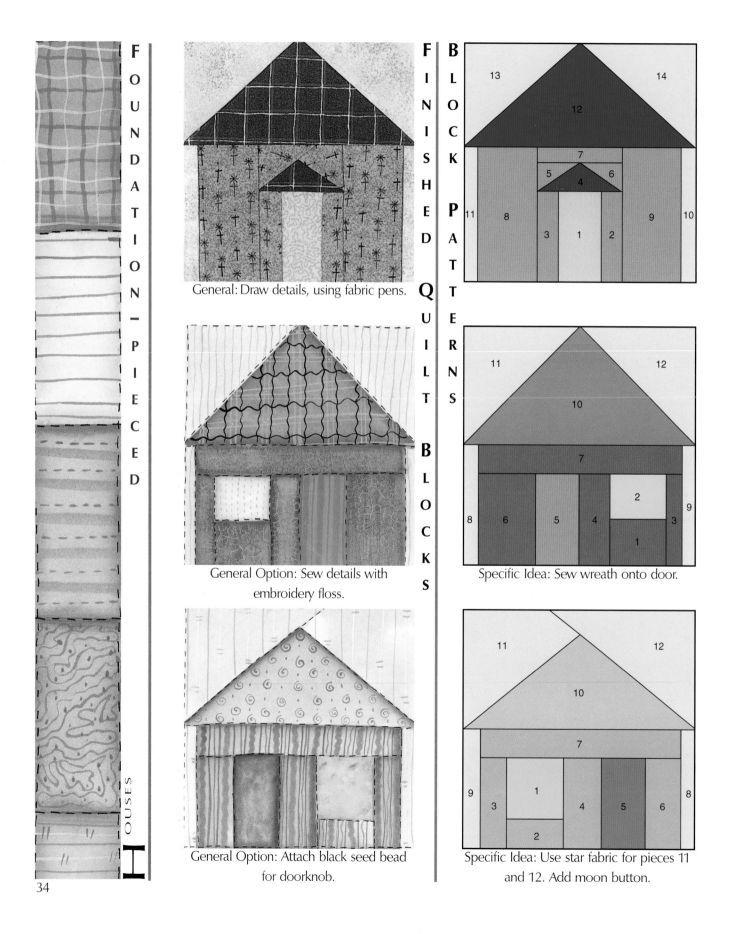

General: Draw details, using fabric pens.

General Option: Sew details with embroidery floss.

General Option: Attach black seed bead for doorknob.

Specific Idea: Sew wreath onto door.

Specific Idea: Use star fabric for pieces 11 and 12. Add moon button.

HOUSES

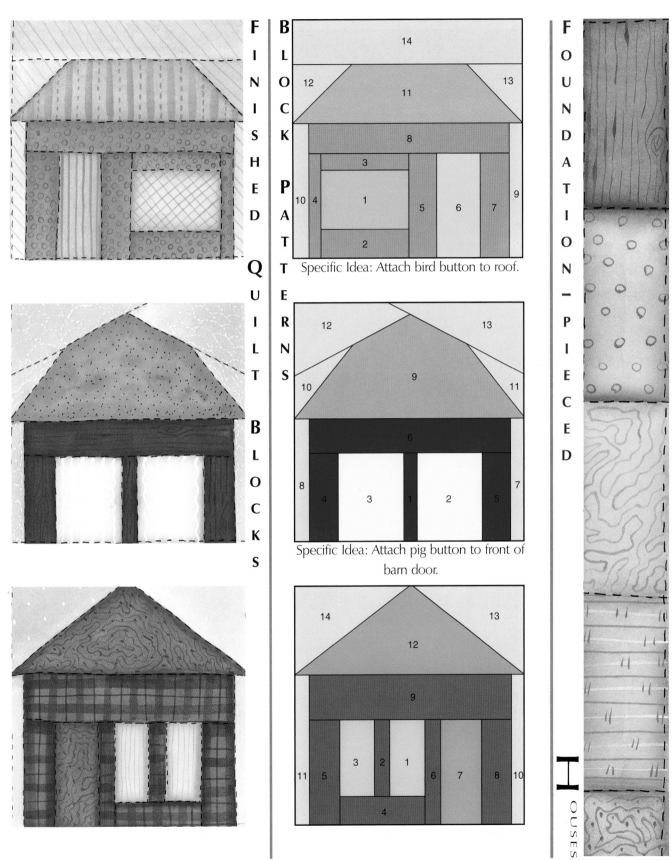

Specific Idea: Attach bird button to roof.

Specific Idea: Attach pig button to front of
barn door.

35

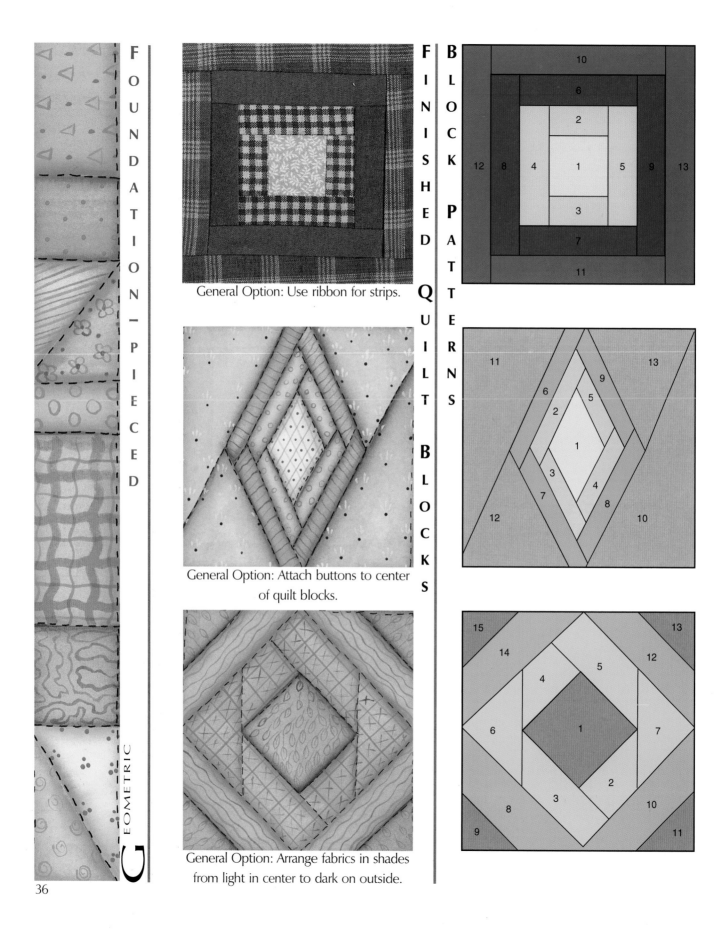

GEOMETRIC

General Option: Use ribbon for strips.

General Option: Attach buttons to center of quilt blocks.

General Option: Arrange fabrics in shades from light in center to dark on outside.

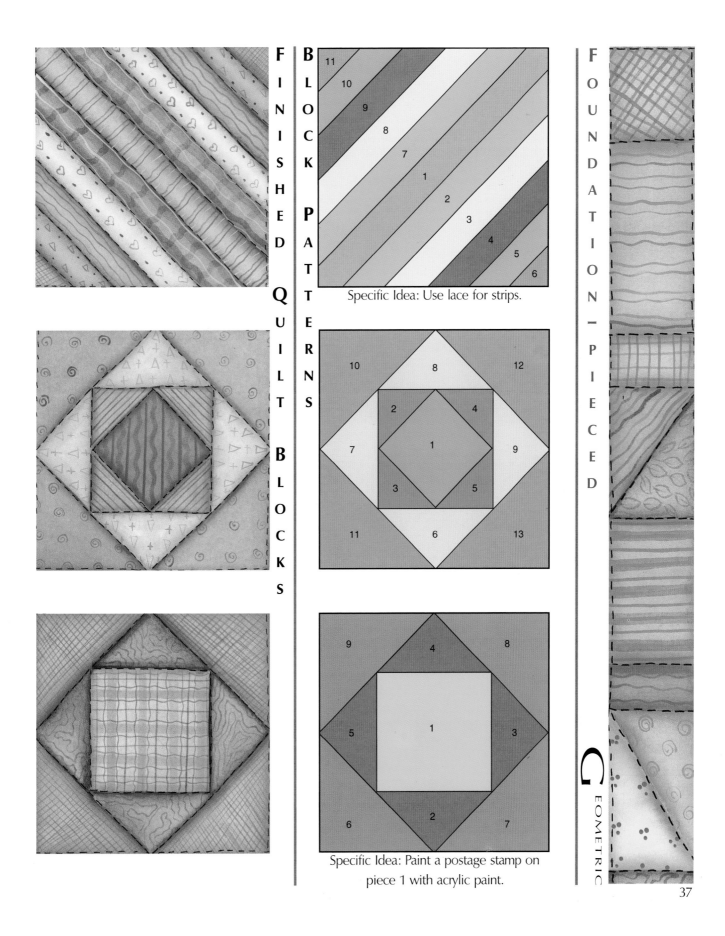

FINISHED QUILT BLOCKS

BLOCK PATTERNS

11
10
9
8
7
1
2
3
4
5
6

Specific Idea: Use lace for strips.

10   8   12
2   4
7   1   9
3   5
11   6   13

9   4   8
5   1   3
6   2   7

Specific Idea: Paint a postage stamp on piece 1 with acrylic paint.

FOUNDATION–PIECED

GEOMETRIC

37

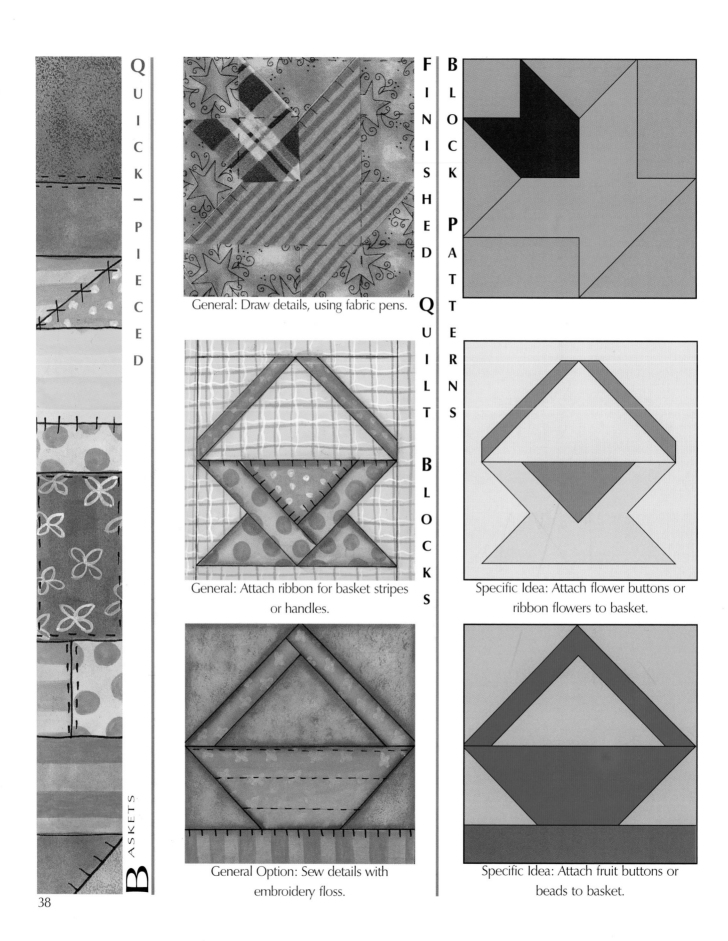

FINISHED QUILT BLOCKS

BLOCK PATTERNS

General: Draw details, using fabric pens.

General: Attach ribbon for basket stripes or handles.

General Option: Sew details with embroidery floss.

Specific Idea: Attach flower buttons or ribbon flowers to basket.

Specific Idea: Attach fruit buttons or beads to basket.

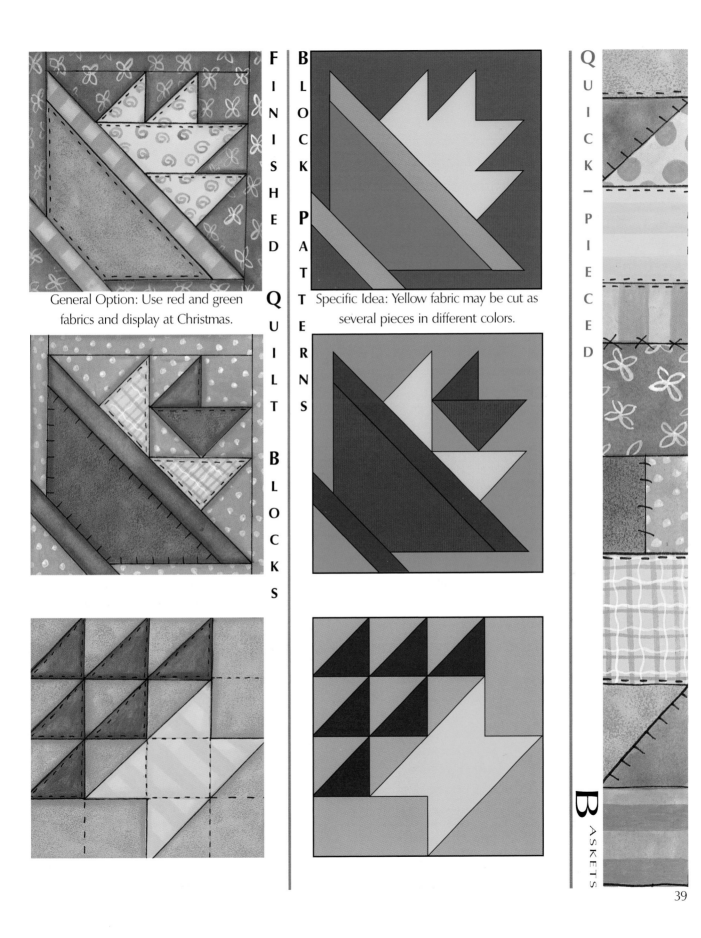

B L O C K   P A T T E R N S

Q U I C K - P I E C E D

General Option: Use red and green fabrics and display at Christmas.

Specific Idea: Yellow fabric may be cut as several pieces in different colors.

B ASKETS

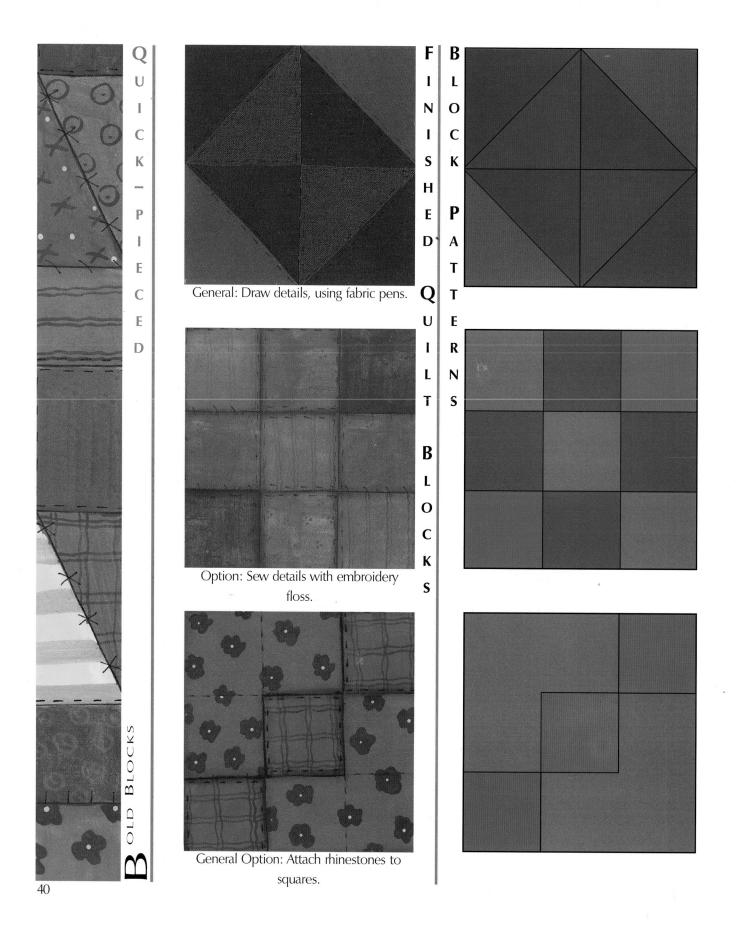

General: Draw details, using fabric pens.

Option: Sew details with embroidery floss.

General Option: Attach rhinestones to squares.

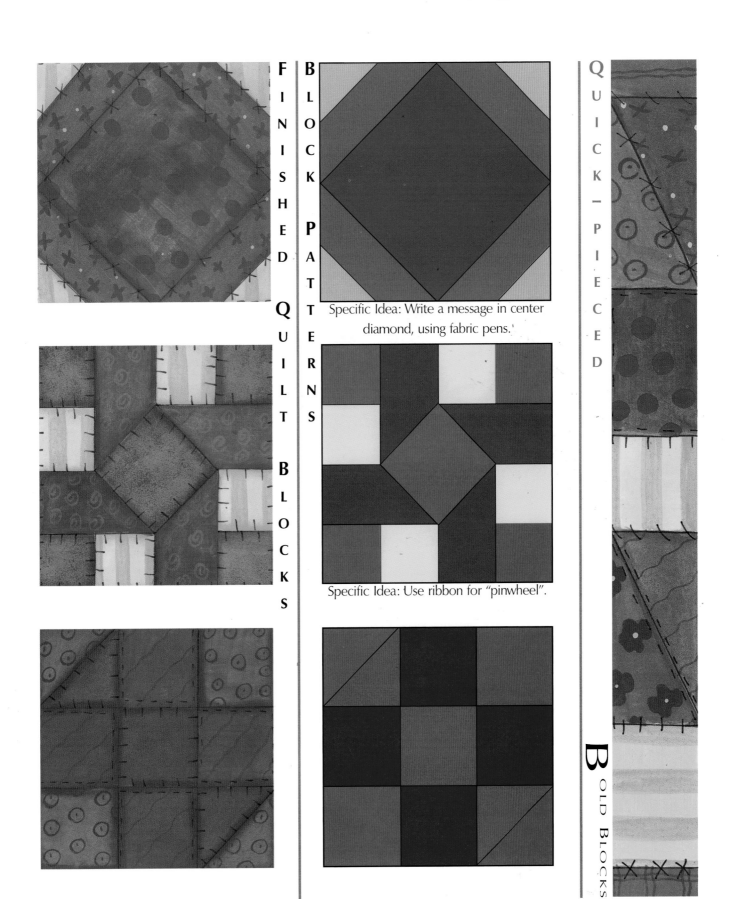

Specific Idea: Write a message in center diamond, using fabric pens.

Specific Idea: Use ribbon for "pinwheel".

BOLD BLOCKS

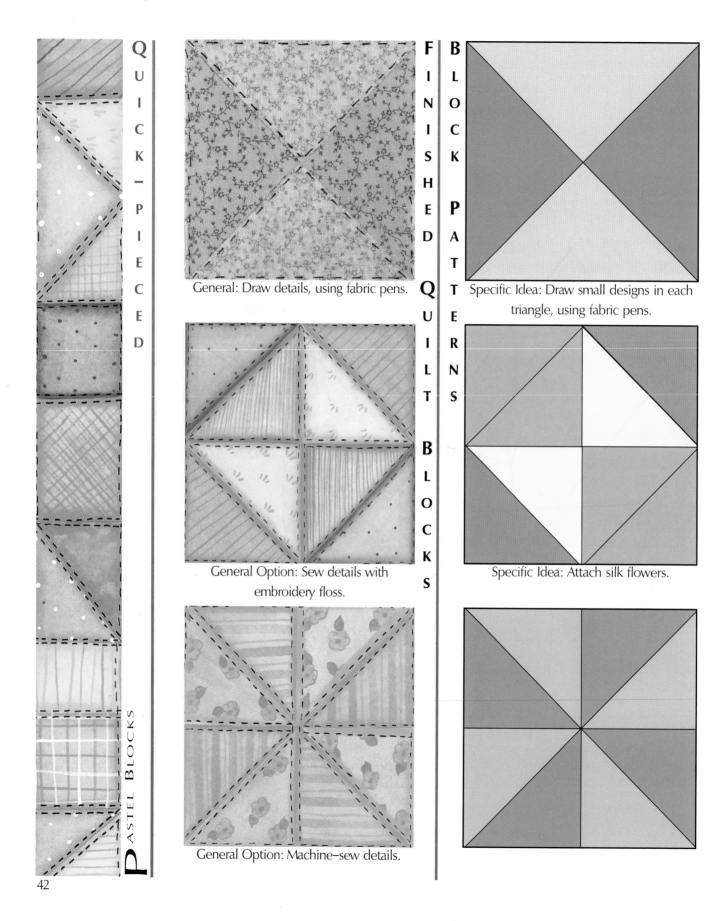

General: Draw details, using fabric pens.

General Option: Sew details with embroidery floss.

General Option: Machine-sew details.

Specific Idea: Draw small designs in each triangle, using fabric pens.

Specific Idea: Attach silk flowers.

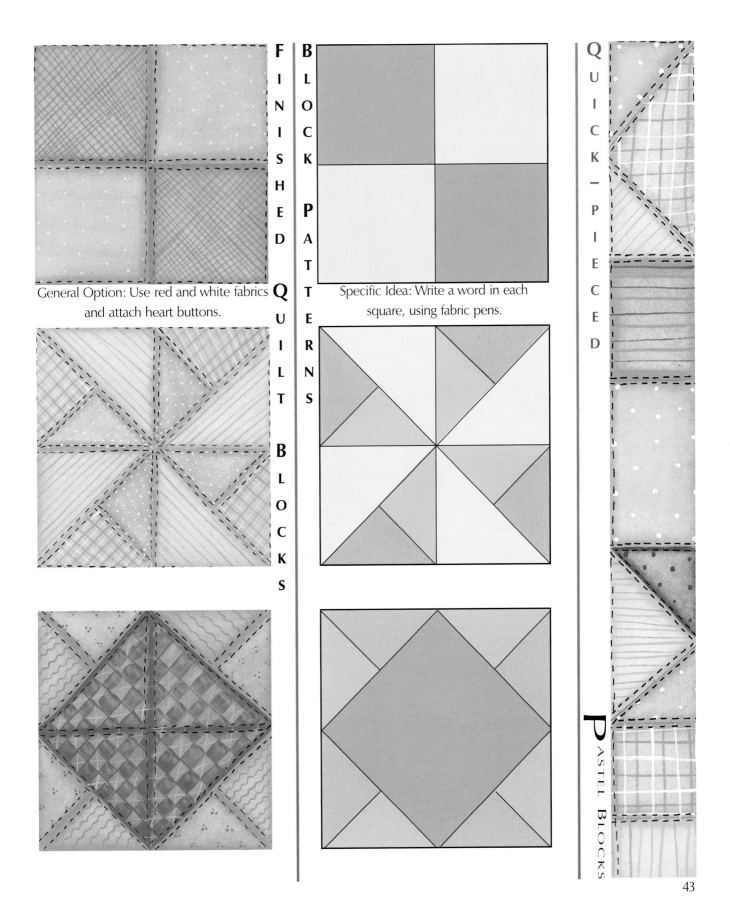

FINISHED QUILT BLOCKS

General Option: Use red and white fabrics and attach heart buttons.

BLOCK PATTERNS

Specific Idea: Write a word in each square, using fabric pens.

QUICK-PIECED PASTEL BLOCKS

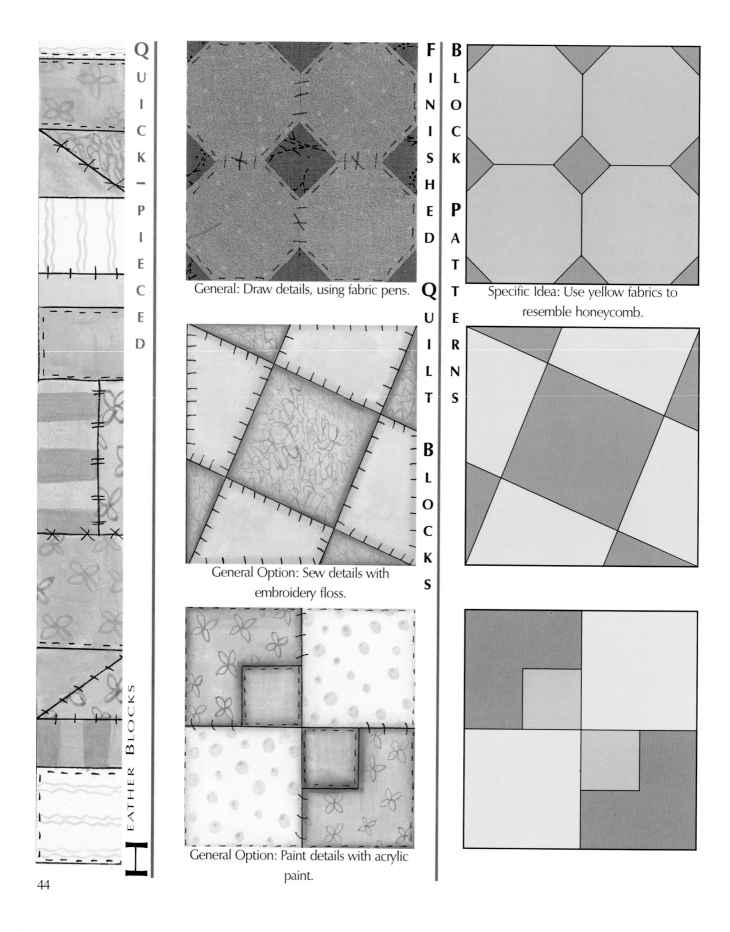

Q U I C K - P I E C E D

F I N I S H E D

Q U I L T

B L O C K S

B L O C K P A T T E R N S

H EATHER B LOCKS

General: Draw details, using fabric pens.

Specific Idea: Use yellow fabrics to resemble honeycomb.

General Option: Sew details with embroidery floss.

General Option: Paint details with acrylic paint.

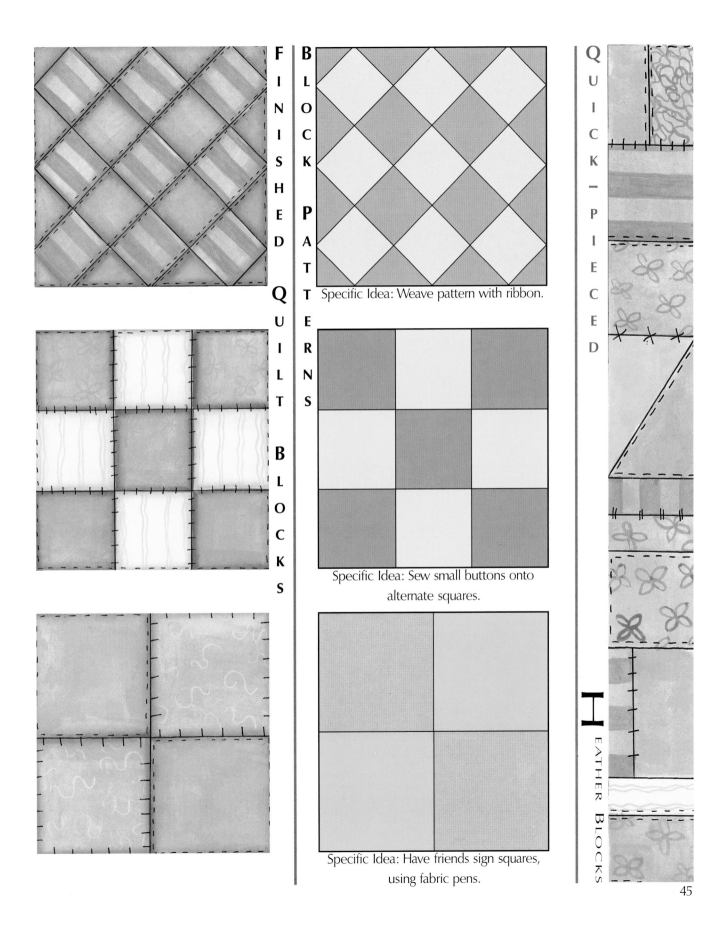

FINISHED QUILT BLOCKS

BLOCK PATTERNS

Specific Idea: Weave pattern with ribbon.

Specific Idea: Sew small buttons onto alternate squares.

Specific Idea: Have friends sign squares, using fabric pens.

QUICK-PIECED

HEATHER BLOCKS

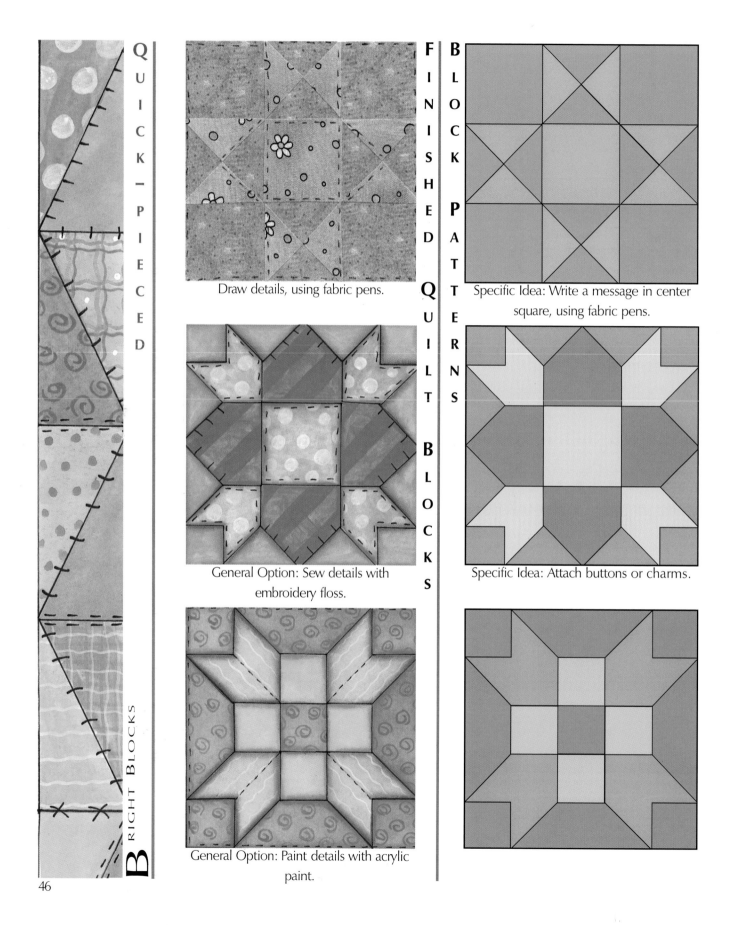

Draw details, using fabric pens.

Specific Idea: Write a message in center square, using fabric pens.

General Option: Sew details with embroidery floss.

Specific Idea: Attach buttons or charms.

General Option: Paint details with acrylic paint.

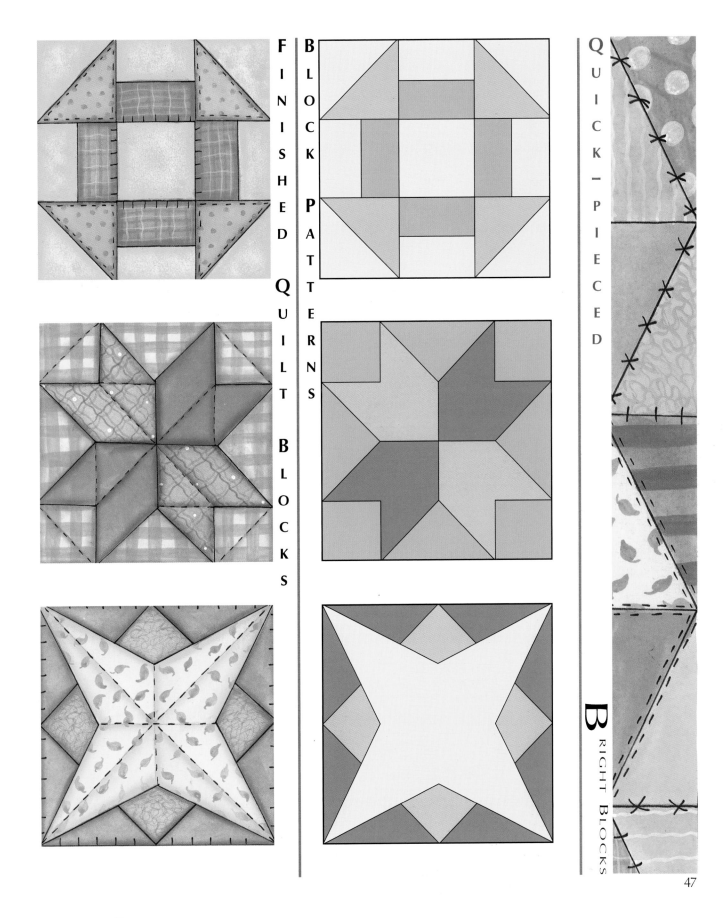

General: Draw details, using fabric pens.

Specific Idea: Attach seed bead for eye.

General Option: Sew details with embroidery floss.

FINISHED QUILT BLOCKS

BLOCK PATTERNS

QUICK-PIECED

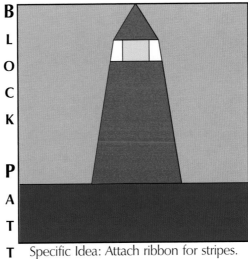

Specific Idea: Attach ribbon for stripes.

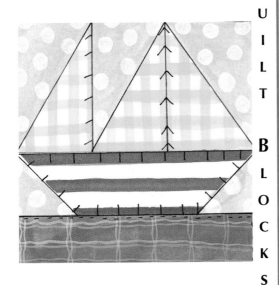

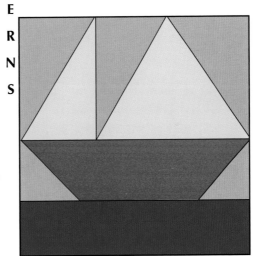

Specific Idea: Write a name on sails, using fabric pen.

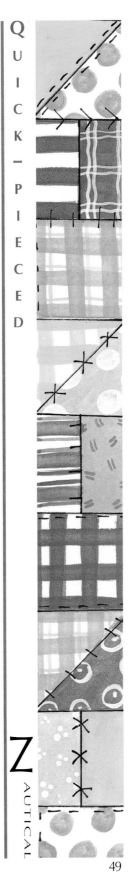

Z
AUTICAL

49

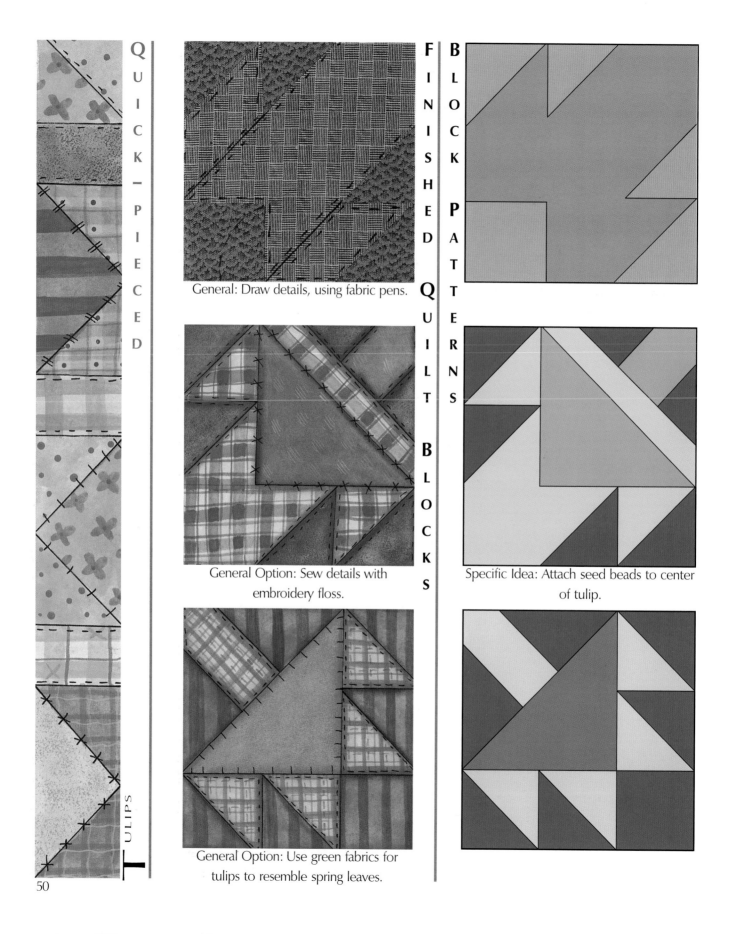

FINISHED QUILT BLOCKS

BLOCK PATTERNS

General: Draw details, using fabric pens.

General Option: Sew details with embroidery floss.

Specific Idea: Attach seed beads to center of tulip.

General Option: Use green fabrics for tulips to resemble spring leaves.

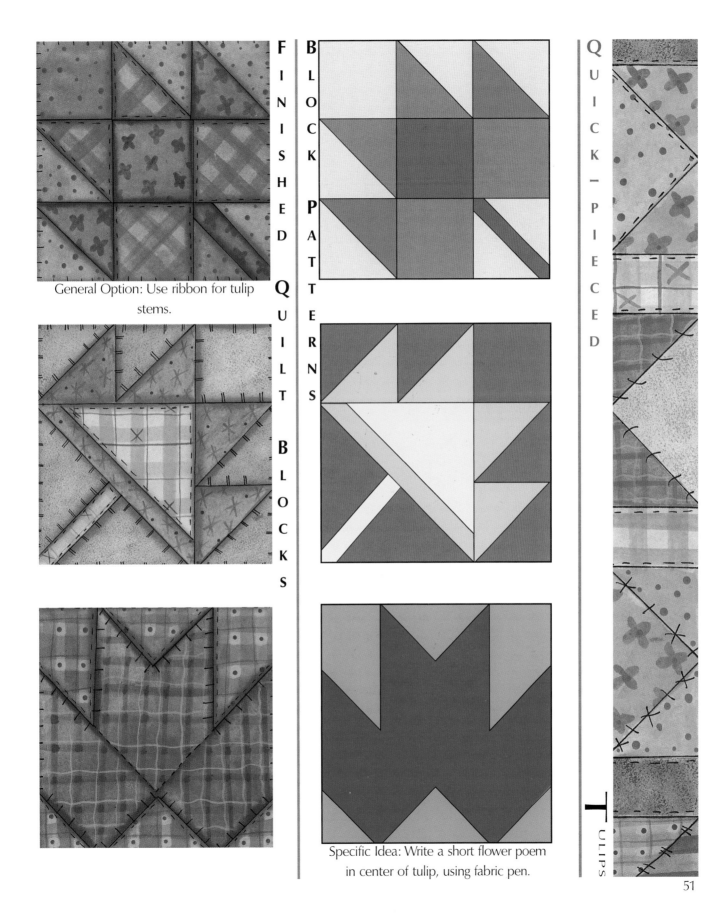

General Option: Use ribbon for tulip stems.

Specific Idea: Write a short flower poem in center of tulip, using fabric pen.

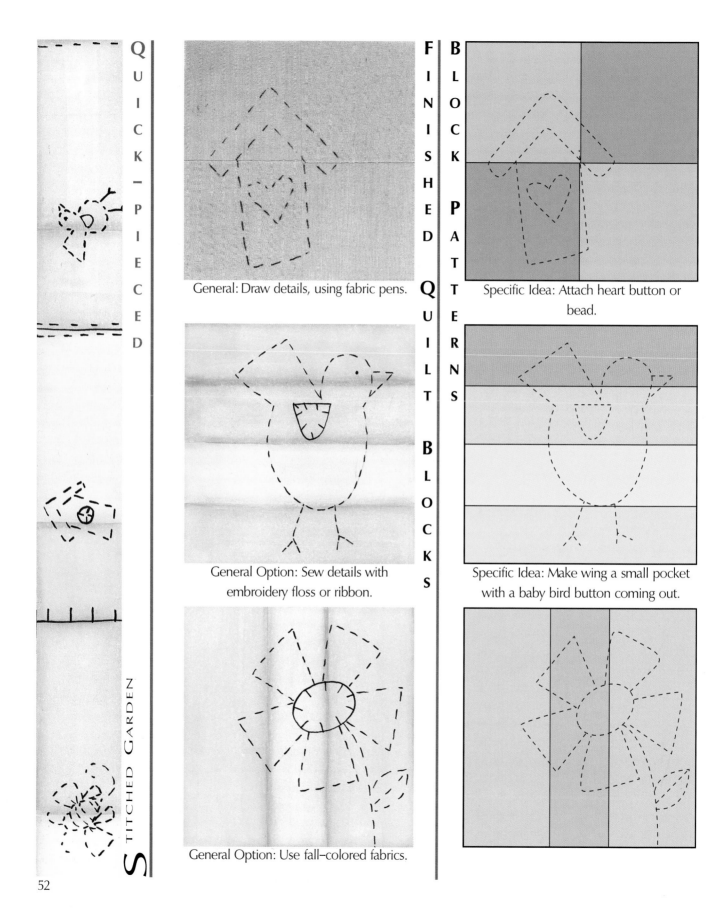

General: Draw details, using fabric pens.

Specific Idea: Attach heart button or bead.

General Option: Sew details with embroidery floss or ribbon.

Specific Idea: Make wing a small pocket with a baby bird button coming out.

General Option: Use fall-colored fabrics.

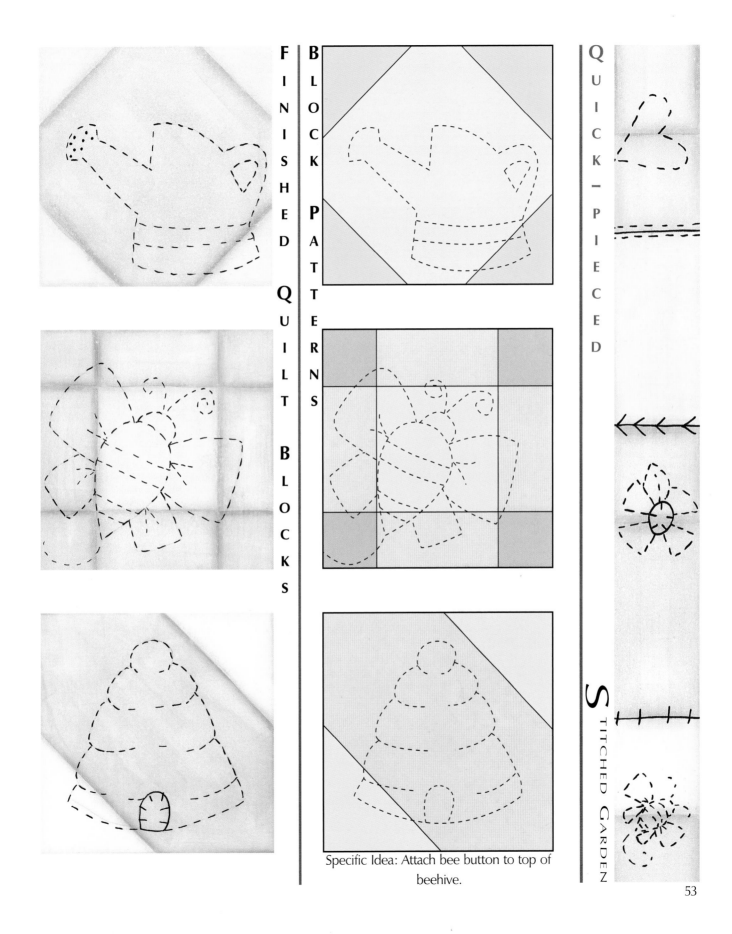

Specific Idea: Attach bee button to top of beehive.

*S*TITCHED GARDEN

FINISHED QUILT BLOCKS

BLOCK PATTERNS

General: Draw details, using fabric pens.

Specific Idea: Use fleece for sheep's coat.

General Option: Sew details with embroidery floss.

Specific Idea: Make a tiny tassel for zebra's tail with embroidery floss.

General Option: Attach seed beads for eyes.

M
ENAGERIE

General: Draw details, using fabric pens.

Specific Idea: Make a tiny tassel for camel's tail with embroidery floss.

General Option: Sew details with embroidery floss.

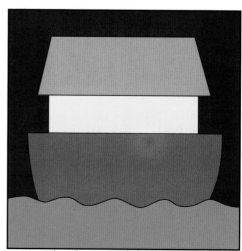

General Option: Use jungle print fabric for background.

Specific Idea: Attach buttons for ark's portholes.

General Option: Sew a french knot with black embroidery floss for animal eyes.

Specific Idea: Make lion's mane with embroidery floss.

Specific Idea: Lightly pad center of turtle's shell with cotton batting.

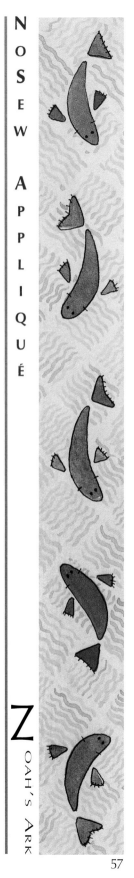

General: Attach buttons for wheels. Draw details, using fabric pens.

General: Paint eyes and markings with fabric paint.

General Option: Use animal print fabric for each animal.

Specific Idea: Make lion's mane and tail with embroidery floss.

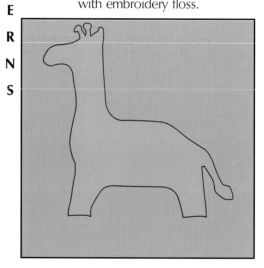

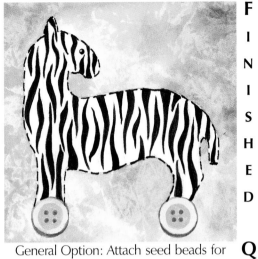

General Option: Attach seed beads for eyes.

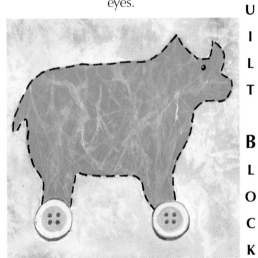

General Option: Use watercolor–like fabrics for backgrounds.

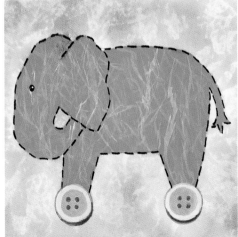

General Option: Use non–traditional colored fabrics for animals.

Specific Idea: Paint zebra's stripes green.

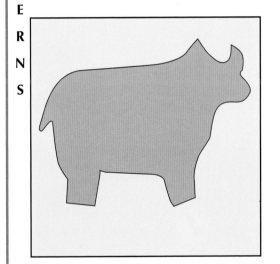

A NIMAL TOYS

General: Draw details, using fabric pens.

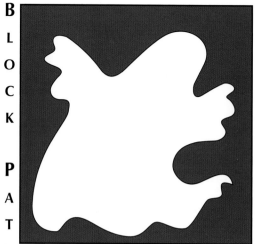

Specific Idea: Attach snaps for ghost's eyes and a heart-shaped button for mouth.

General Option: Sew details with embroidery floss.

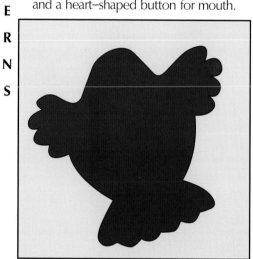

Specific Idea: Attach bugle beads for bird's feet.

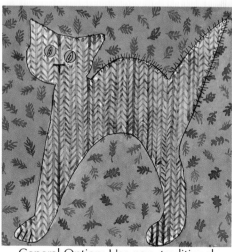

General Option: Use non-traditional Halloween colors for backgrounds.

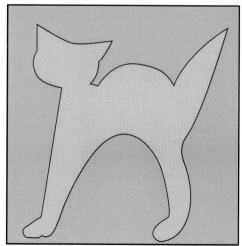

Specific Idea: Attach buttons for cat's eyes.

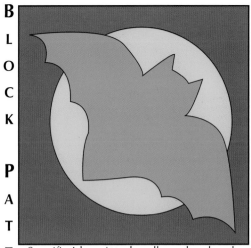

Specific Idea: Attach yellow glass beads for bat's eyes.

Specific Idea: Paint pumpkin's eyes and mouth with florescent paint.

Specific Idea: Make witch's broom with embroidery floss.

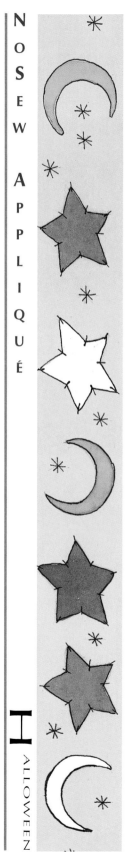

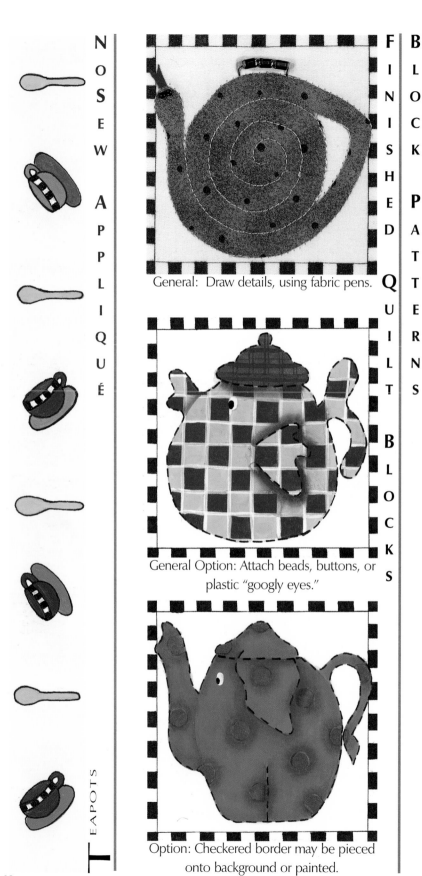

General: Draw details, using fabric pens.

General Option: Attach beads, buttons, or plastic "googly eyes."

Option: Checkered border may be pieced onto background or painted.

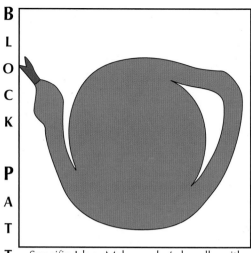

Specific Idea: Make snake's handle with wire and beads. Machine sew coils.

Specific Idea: Lightly pad center of lid with cotton batting.

TEAPOTS

62

BLOCK PATTERNS

NO SEW APPLIQUÉ

Specific Idea: Make turtle's handle with wire and beads.

TEAPOTS

General: Draw details, using fabric pens.

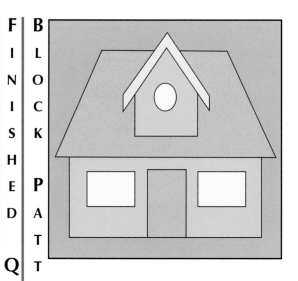

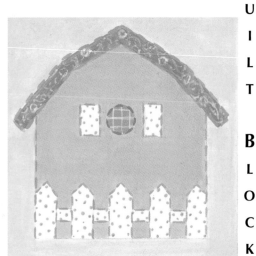

General Option: Paint backstitch lines with fabric "puff" paint.

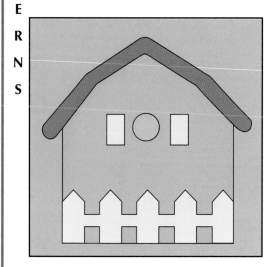

General Option: Use red and green Christmas fabrics for birdhouses.

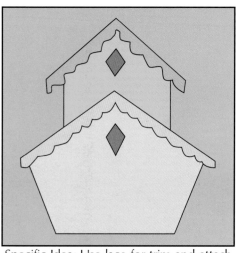

Specific Idea: Use lace for trim and attach jewels for "holes".

Specific Idea: Attach bead for top of birdhouse.

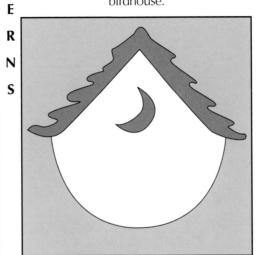

Specific Idea: Attach moon button for "hole".

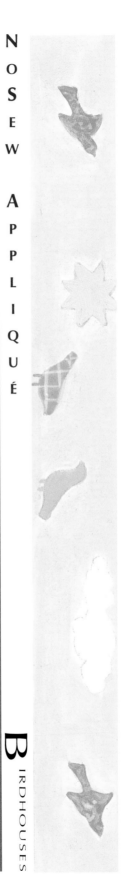

65

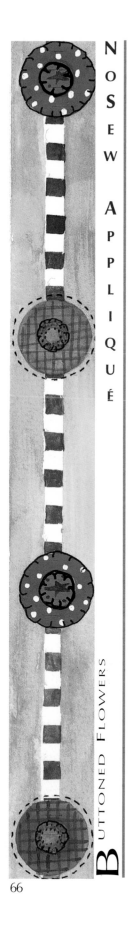

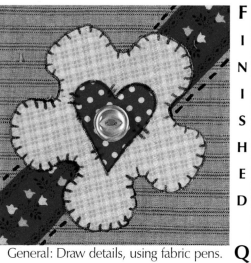

General: Draw details, using fabric pens.

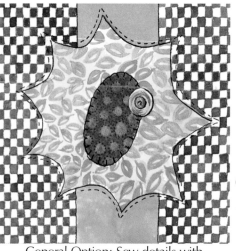

General Option: Sew details with embroidery floss.

General Option: Attach button to flower center.

Specific Idea: Sew on button with silk floss.

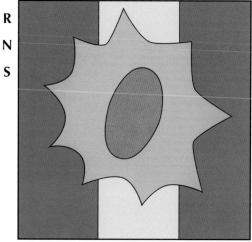

Specific Idea: Use ribbon for stripe behind flower.

N O S E W   A P P L I Q U É

B UTTONED FLOWERS

F I N I S H E D   Q U I L T   B L O C K S

B L O C K   P A T T E R N S

66

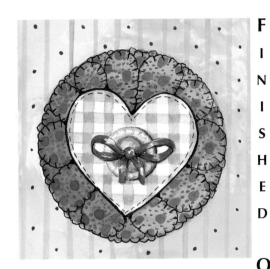

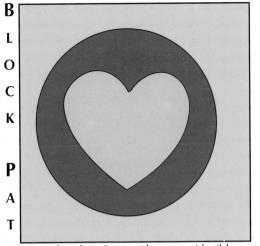

Specific Idea: Sew on button with ribbon and tie in bow.

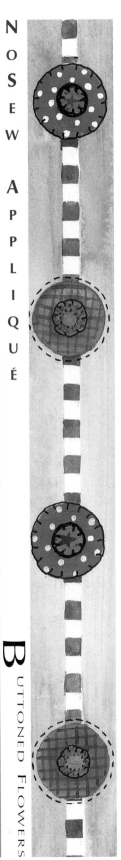

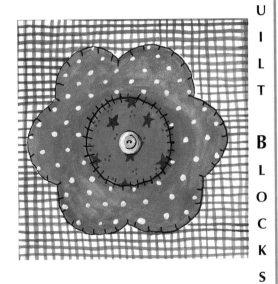

Specific Idea: Use lace doily for flower center.

BUTTONED FLOWERS

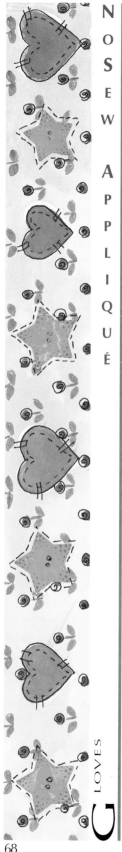

General: Draw details, using fabric pens.

Specific Idea: Attach bow and charm.

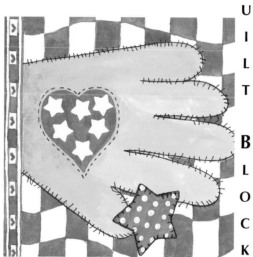

General Option: Tea dye muslin for background fabric.

Specific Idea: Attach buttons or charms for heart and star.

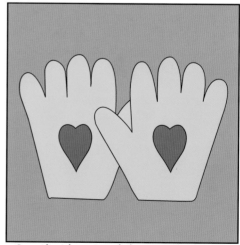

Specific Idea: Attach buttons for hearts.

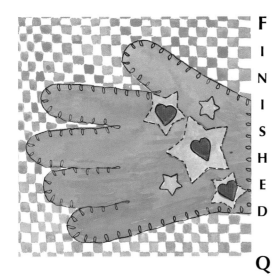

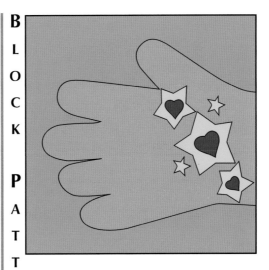

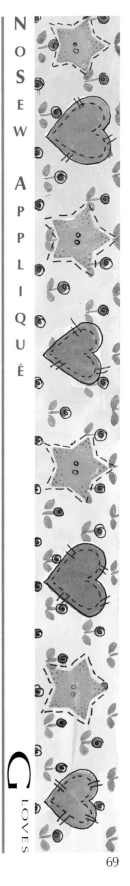

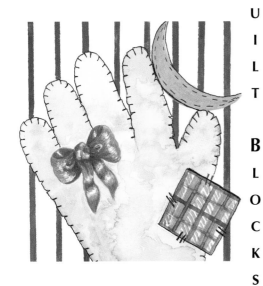

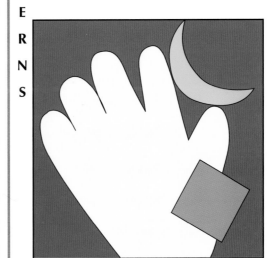

Specific Idea: Tea–dye muslin for glove.

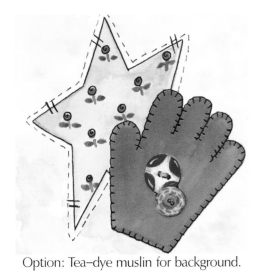

Option: Tea–dye muslin for background.

69

General: Draw details, using fabric pens.

General: Attach buttons.

General: Add blush, using a worn paint-
brush, a little fabric paint, and a light touch.

General Option: Adhere real twigs with fabric glue for arms.

Specific Idea: Use doll skates instead of fabric cutouts.

Specific Idea: Use ribbon rose for flower on snowman's hat.

Specific Idea: Make broom from raffia and a stick. Adhere with fabric glue.

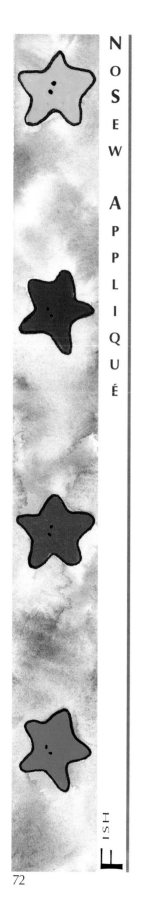

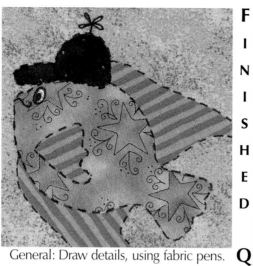

General: Draw details, using fabric pens.

General Option: Sew details with embroidery floss.

Specific Idea: Use ribbon for bowtie.

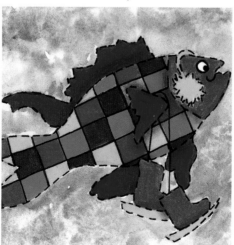

General Option: Paint eyes with fabric paint.

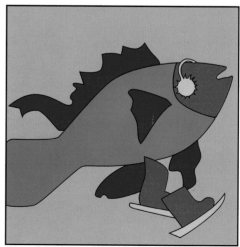

Specific Idea: Use pom–pom for earmuff.

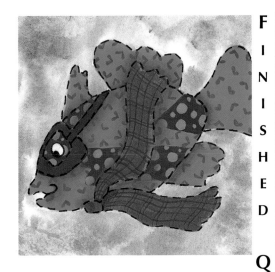

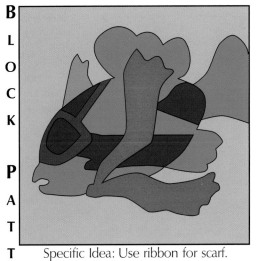

Specific Idea: Use ribbon for scarf.

General Option: Use plastic "googly eyes."

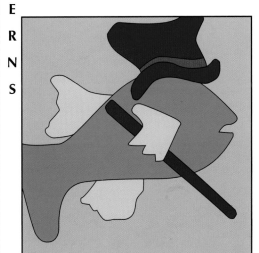

Specific Idea: Use painted dowel for walking stick.

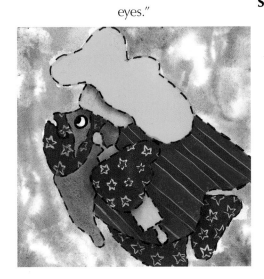

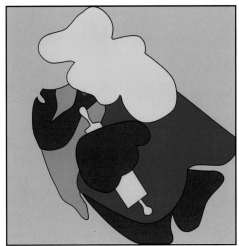

Specific Idea: Lightly pad top of chef's hat with cotton batting.

BUTTON-HEAD CLOWNS

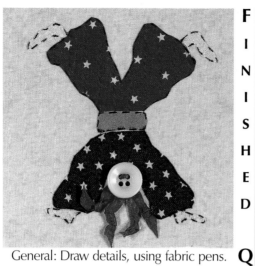

General: Draw details, using fabric pens.

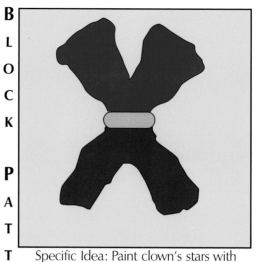

Specific Idea: Paint clown's stars with
fabric "glitter" paint.

General: Attach button for head.

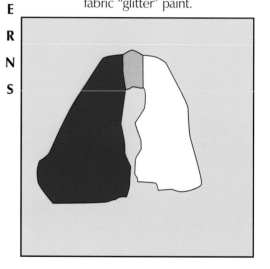

General: Sew on red silk ribbon for mouth
and hair.

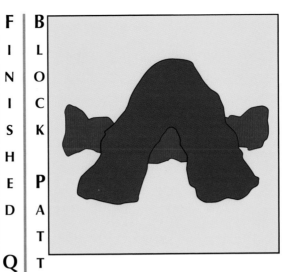

General option: Sew details with embroidery floss.

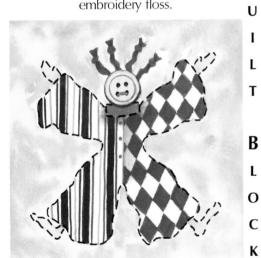

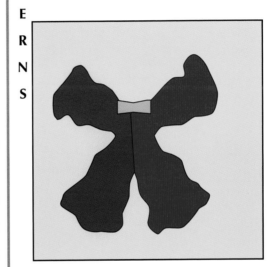

General Option: Paint hands and feet with peach "puff" paint.

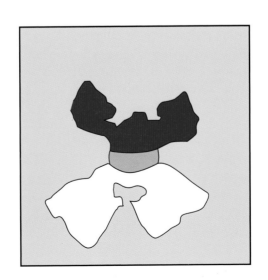

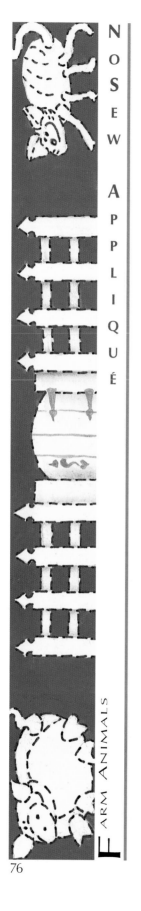

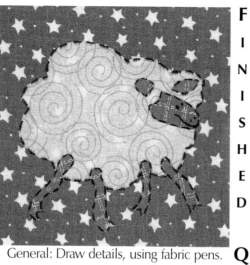

General: Draw details, using fabric pens.

Specific Idea: Use "fuzzy" fabric for sheep's coat.

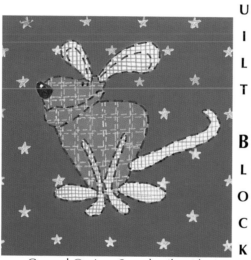

General Option: Sew details with embroidery floss.

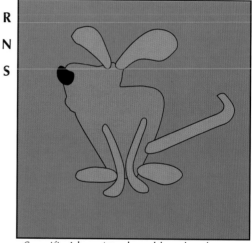

Specific Idea: Attach red bead or button for dog's nose.

General Option: Attach seed beads for eyes.

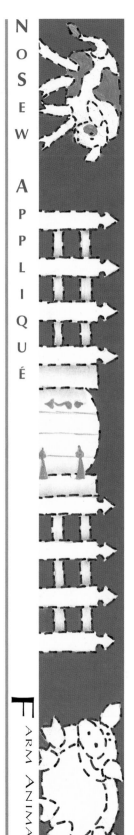

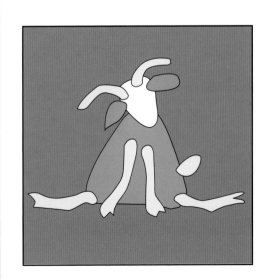

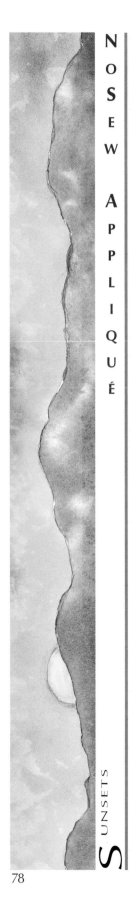

78

General: Stamp foliage onto foreground, using rubber stamps with permanent ink.

General Option: Stamps may be touched up, using fabric pens.

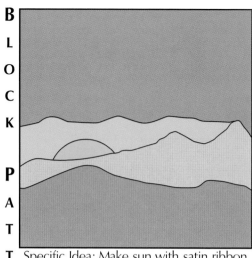

Specific Idea: Make sun with satin ribbon.

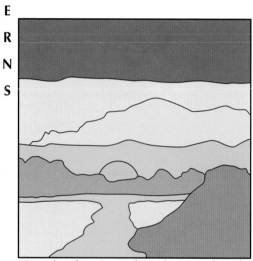

Specific Idea: Sew a lazy daisy stitch with embroidery floss for tree's leaves.

B L O C K P A T T E R N S

Specific Idea: Attach tiny bird buttons
to sky.

N O S E W A P P L I Q U É

S UNSETS

79

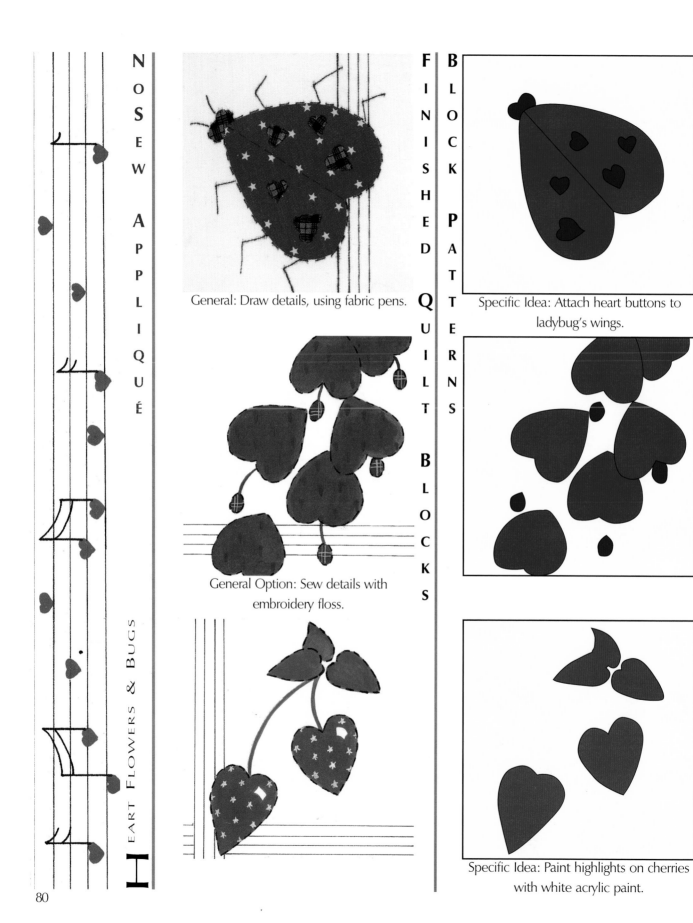

HEART FLOWERS & BUGS

General: Draw details, using fabric pens.

General Option: Sew details with embroidery floss.

FINISHED QUILT BLOCKS

BLOCK PATTERNS

Specific Idea: Attach heart buttons to ladybug's wings.

Specific Idea: Paint highlights on cherries with white acrylic paint.

H EART FLOWERS & BUGS

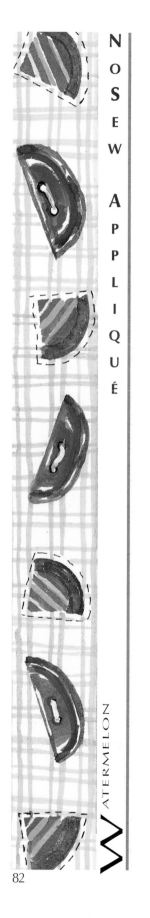

General: Draw details, using fabric pens.

Specific: Draw cherry stems, using a cream fabric pen.

General Option: Sew details with embroidery floss.

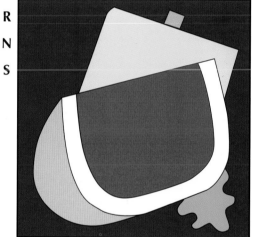

Specific: Paint watermelon sign with acrylic paint.

General Option: Use red and green fabrics and display at Christmas.

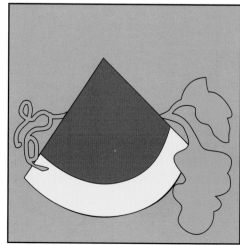

Specific: Paint green rind with acrylic paint.

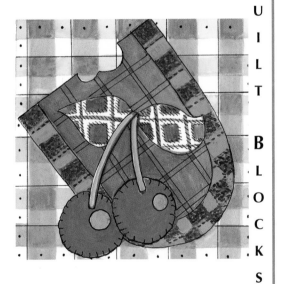

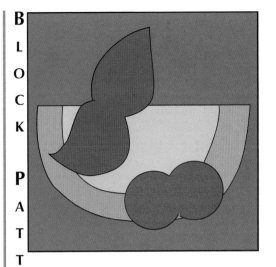

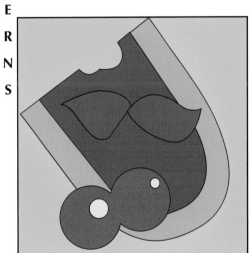

Specific Idea: Use satin cord for cherry's stems.

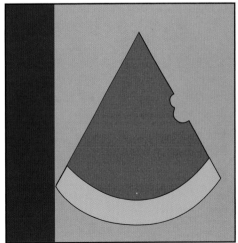

Specific Idea: Use ribbon border for checkered stripe.

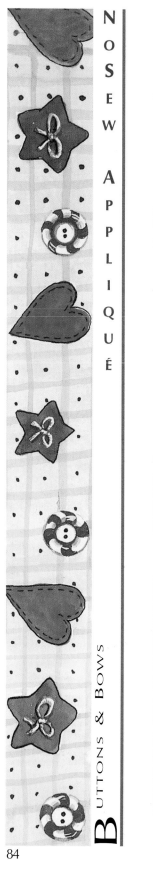

General: Draw details, using fabric pens.

General: Attach buttons and bows.

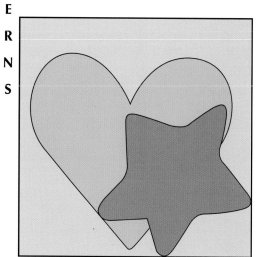

Specific Idea: Lightly pad star's center with cotton batting.

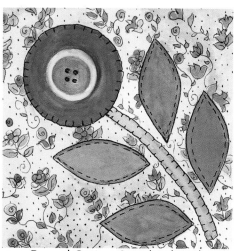

General Option: Sew details with embroidery floss.

Specific Idea: Use brightly dyed doily for flower.

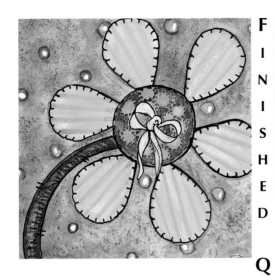

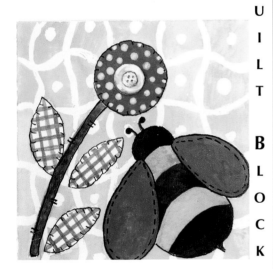

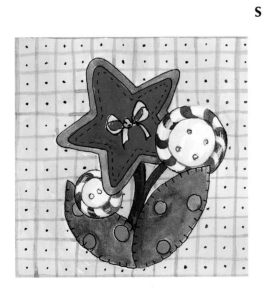

Specific Idea: Dot leaves with fabric paint.

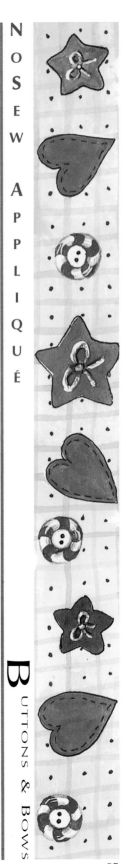

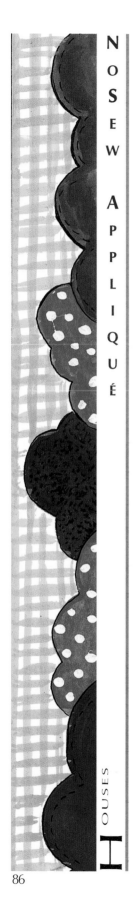

General: Draw details, using fabric pens.

General Option: Sew details with
embroidery floss.

Specific Idea: Attach heart bead or button
for "window" over door.

General Option: Patterns may be made
into stencils.

Specific Idea: Attach red beads for tree's
"apples".

Specific Idea: Attach button for "window" over door.

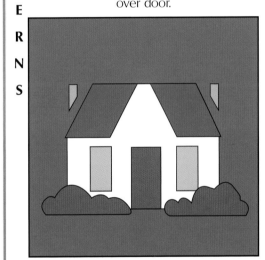

Specific Idea: Attach ribbon roses to hedge.

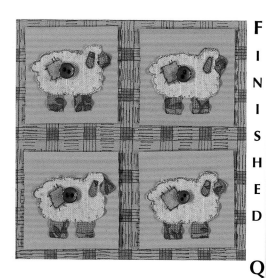

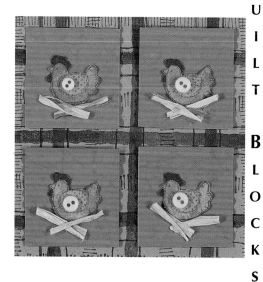

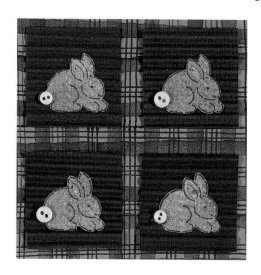

FINISHED QUILT BLOCKS

FINISHED QUILT BLOCKS

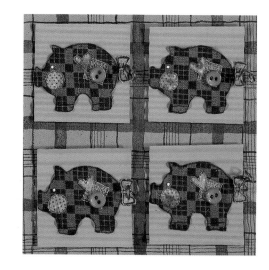

1. Stamp animals on fabric. Color animals, using fabric pens, then cut out. Apply liquid fray preventive to edges.

2. Adhere animals onto ¾" colored, corrugated paper squares with fabric glue. Adhere ¾" squares onto 4" background fabric with fabric glue.

3. Embellish with buttons and bows.

1. Emboss design on tracing paper, using rubber stamp and embossing powder.

2. Place embossed side of tracing paper on right side of fabric.

3. Iron on low to medium setting for one to two seconds.

Note: Overheating design while ironing will melt embossing into fabric.

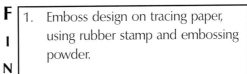

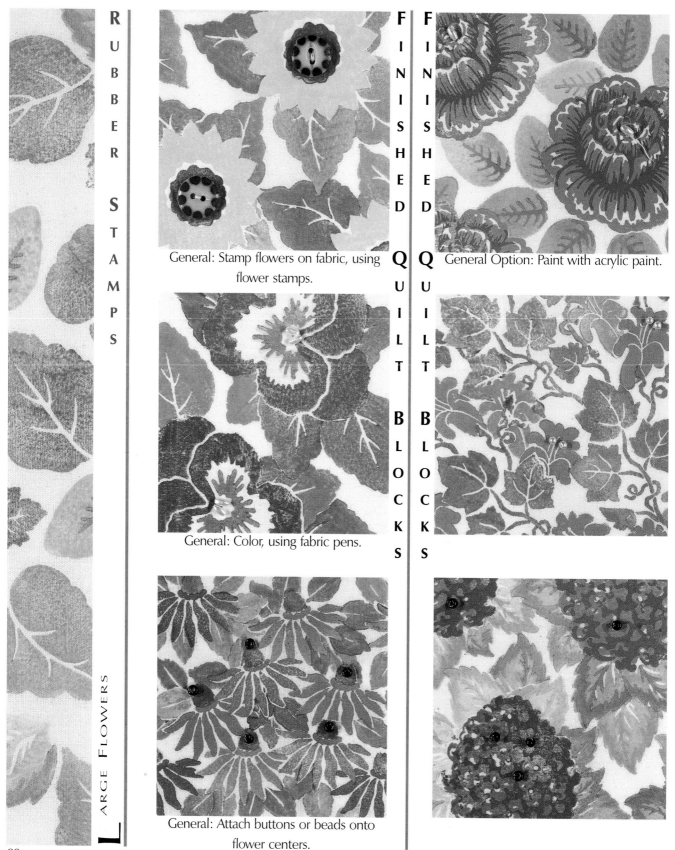

General: Stamp flowers on fabric, using flower stamps.

General Option: Paint with acrylic paint.

General: Color, using fabric pens.

General: Attach buttons or beads onto flower centers.

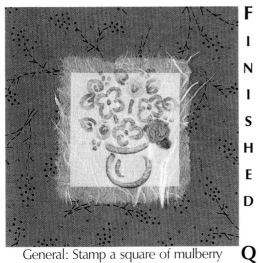

F
I
N
I
S
H
E
D

Q
U
I
L
T

B
L
O
C
K
S

General: Stamp a square of mulberry paper and appliqué onto fabric.

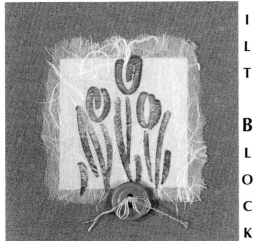

General: Attach buttons and ribbon, jute or fabric bows onto designs.

F
I
N
I
S
H
E
D

Q
U
I
L
T

B
L
O
C
K
S

Specific: Appliqué ribbon between mulberry paper and background fabric.

R
U
B
B
E
R

S
T
A
M
P
S

S MALL FLOWERS

General: Tape stencil(s) to fabric. Color, using stencil pens.

General: Draw details, using fabric pens.

General: Sew on buttons with embroidery floss and tie floss in bows.

Specific Idea: Attach heart buttons for flower centers.

Specific Idea: Attach ribbon flowers.

Specific Idea: Attach shaped ceramic buttons for birds and bees.

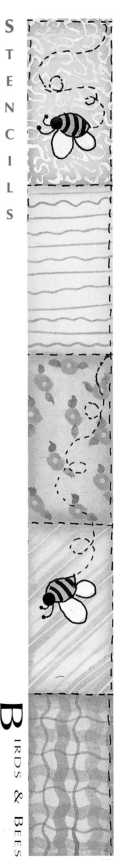

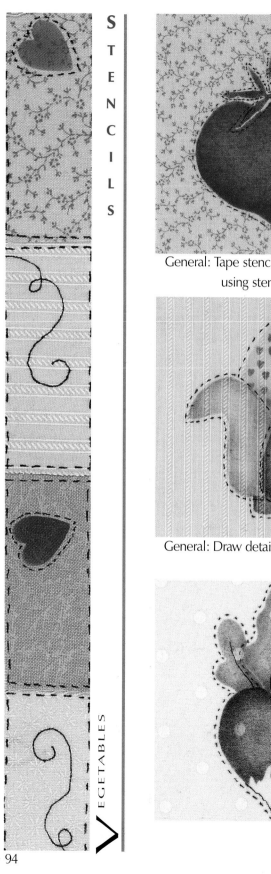

General: Tape stencil(s) to fabric. Color, using stencil pens.

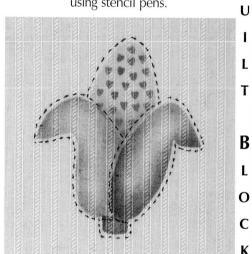

General: Draw details, using fabric pens.

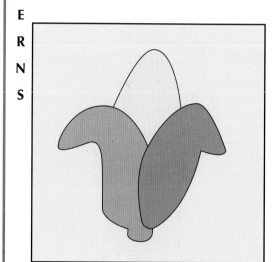

Specific Idea: Make holes in cardstock, using a heart paperpunch for kernels.

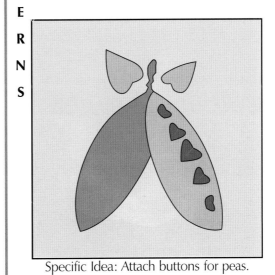

Specific Idea: Attach buttons for peas.

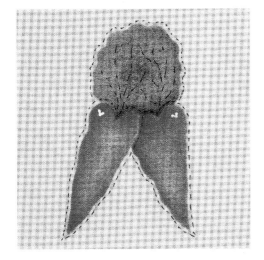

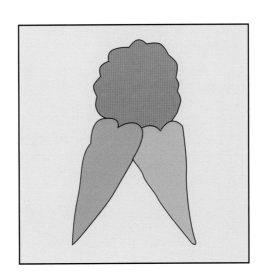

General: Tape stencil(s) to fabric. Color, using stencil pens.

General: Draw details, using fabric pens.

General: Embellish with charms and embroidery floss bows.

Specific: Draw wooly swirls, using black fabric pen.

FARM ANIMALS

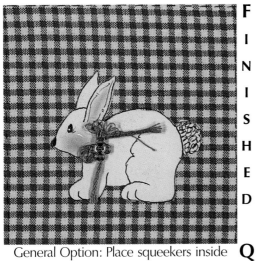

General Option: Place squeekers inside batting to make a fun children's quilt.

BLOCK PATTERNS

Specific Idea: Attach pom–pom for bunny's tail.

Specific Idea: Coil copper wire around a pencil and attach for pig's tail.

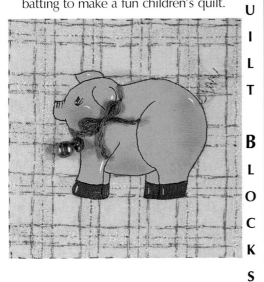

Specific Idea: Make hen's nest with embroidery floss.

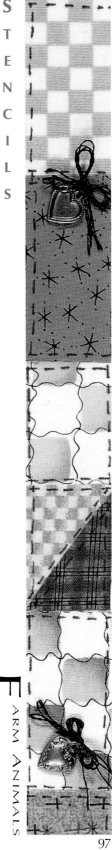

STENCILS

FARM ANIMALS

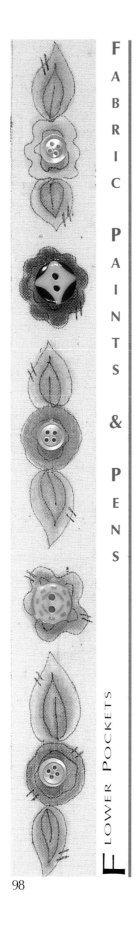

General: Tea–dye muslin. Transfer pattern onto fabric. Color, using fabric pens.

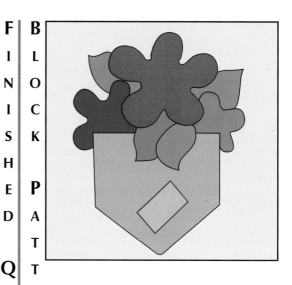

General: Attach buttons to flowers.

General Option: Sew details with embroidery floss.

Specific Idea: Make patch from a small fabric scrap.

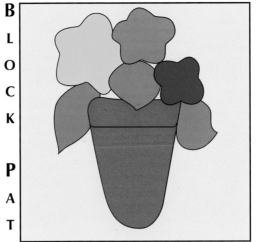

Specific Idea: Attach heart–shaped buttons for flower centers.

Specific Idea: Attach birdhouse button for birdhouse.

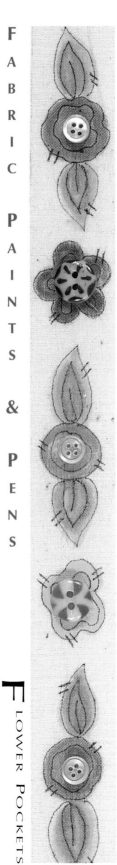

General: Paint with fabric paint. Outline motifs, using fabric pens.

General: Make bows with embroidery floss. Attach buttons and bows.

Specific Idea: Attach bird button to top of center flower.

General Option: These patterns may be cut from fabric and appliquéd.

Specific Idea: Sew button onto basket with embroidery floss.

Specific Idea: Attach small ribbon flowers.

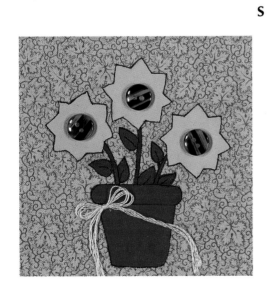

Specific Idea: Attach heart buttons for
flower centers.

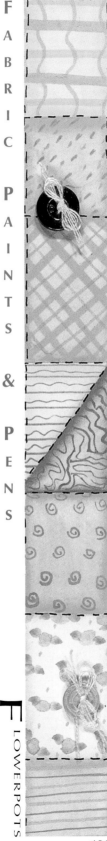

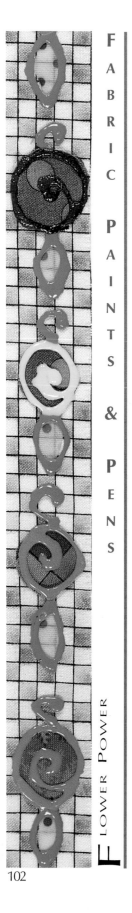

FLOWER POWER

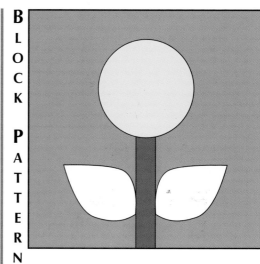

1. Appliqué motif onto background fabric. Leaves are made with adhesive ribbon.

2. Add details with florescent or glitter "puff" paint. Outline leaves first.

3. Turn square around so flower is facing down. Paint flower, working from center to outer edge.

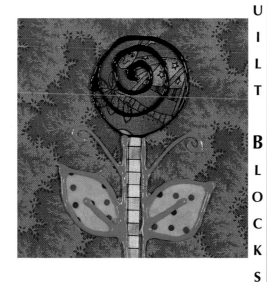

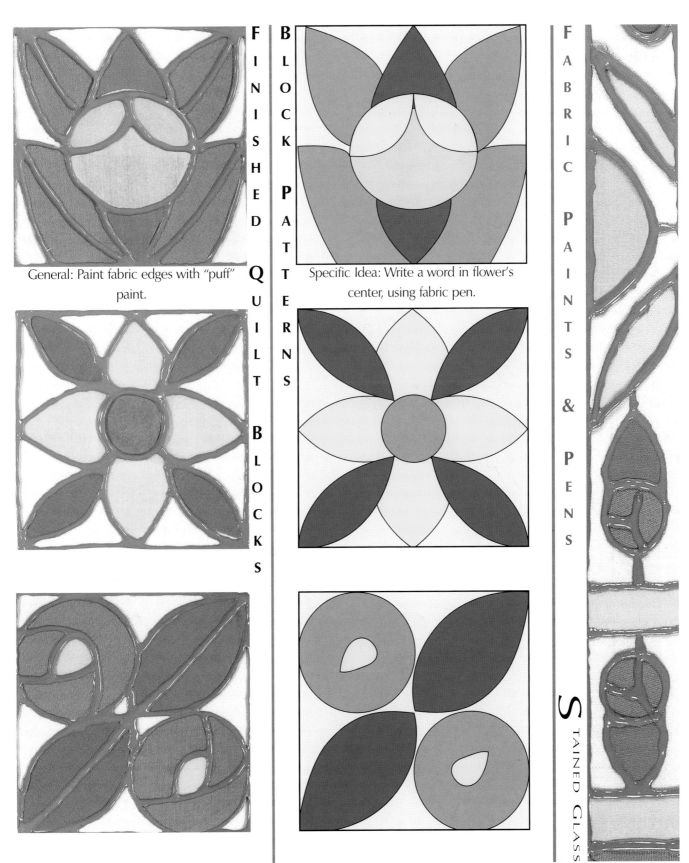

General: Paint fabric edges with "puff" paint.

Specific Idea: Write a word in flower's center, using fabric pen.

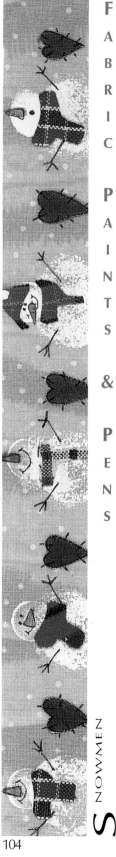

This snowman is an optional design that can be adapted from the pattern below.

1. Sponge snowman design on background fabric with white fabric paint.

2. Appliqué fabric noses, hats, hearts, and muffs.

3. Draw details, using fabric pens.

General Option: Use real twigs for arms.

General Option: Use buttons for hearts.

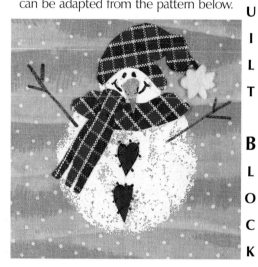

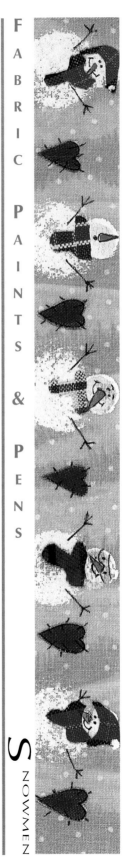

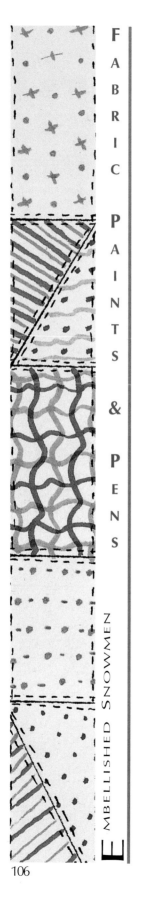

This snowman is an optional design that can be adapted from the pattern below.

1. Transfer pattern onto fabric. Outline, using black fabric pen. Color, using fabric pens.

2. Draw details, using fabric pens onto background fabric.

3. Add blush, using a worn paint-brush, a little fabric paint, and a light touch.

General Option: Sew "threads" with embroidery floss. Use buttons for birds, birdhouses, mittens, etc.

Snowball 5¢

Worms

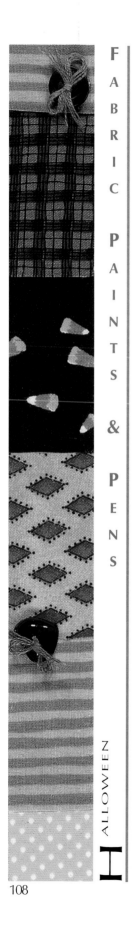

General: Draw pattern, using black fabric pen. Color, using fabric pens.

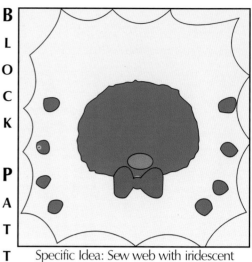

Specific Idea: Sew web with iridescent embroidery floss or fishing line.

General: Blush cheeks with face blush and a cotton swab.

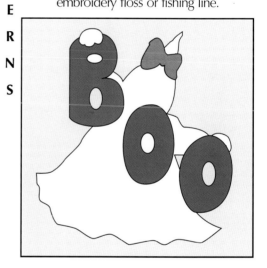

General Option: Paint on top of drawn lines with glitter paint.

Specific: Use short, choppy strokes for fur.

Specific Idea: Use ribbon for bowtie.

Angel Dolls

Materials & Tools

Acrylic paint: red, black
Batting
Decorative trim wire: 4″
Doll hair or mohair
Fabric: cotton, pink, print, solid
Fabric scissors
Hot–glue gun
Liquid fray preventive
Ribbon: 1½″–wide, wire edge (6″)
Sewing needle
Sewing thread: coordinating color
Small paint brush

Diagram 1

1. Organize all materials and tools needed for project. Cut out a 2″ diameter circle of pink cotton fabric. Paint a face, on right side of fabric, below center, with acrylic paint. Place a 1″ diameter circle of batting on wrong side of fabric and tie fabric as shown in Diagram 1.

2. Adhere doll hair onto head with hot glue.

3. Cut and gather–stitch the long side of a 2½″ x 2″ piece of print fabric for angel dress as shown in Diagram 2. Turn edges inside. Tie gathered edge of dress to neck with thread.

4. Fold a 4″ length of 1½″ wide ribbon, overlapping ends. Tie in center as shown in Diagram 3.

5. Cut and gather–stitch the center of a 4″ x 1½″ piece of print fabric for angel sleeves as shown in Diagram 2. Set aside. Cut 4″ x 4″ solid fabric for background. Finish edges with liquid fray preventive. Make a halo with decorative wire.

7. Adhere wings onto back of doll body with hot glue. Repeat for arms and halo. Adhere doll onto 4″ x 4″ background fabric with hot glue. Adhere fabric or button stars.

Diagram 2

2½″ x 2″

4″ x 1½″

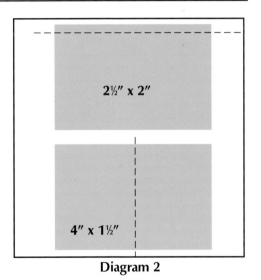

Diagram 3

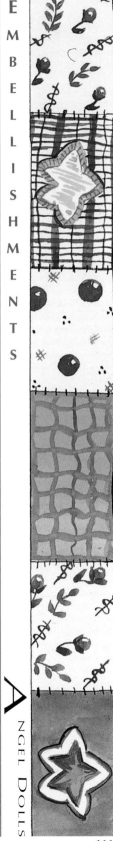

EMBELLISHMENTS

ANGEL DOLLS

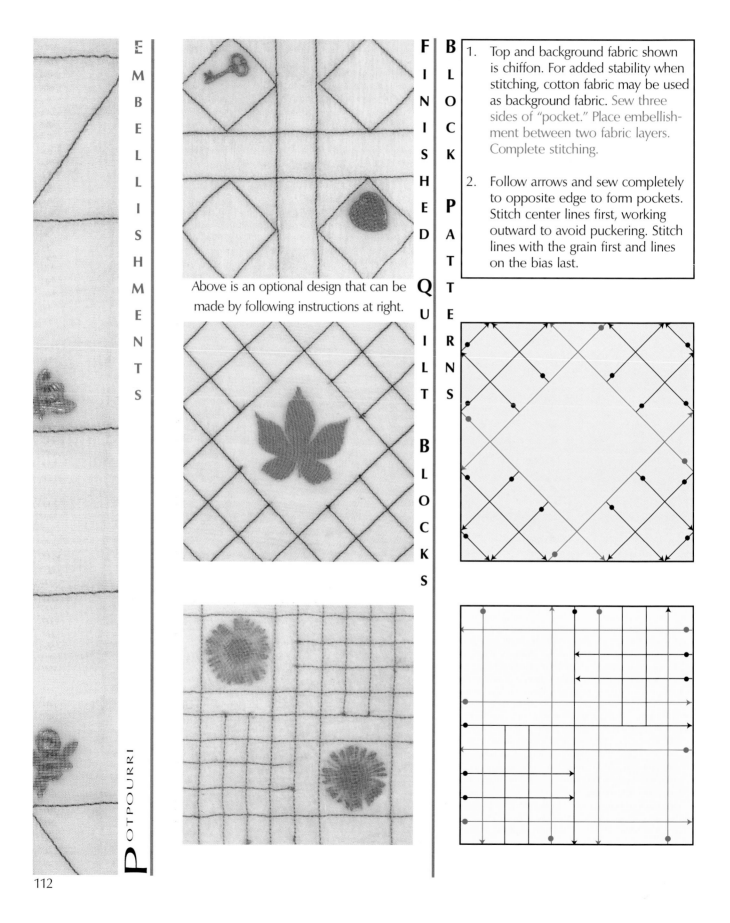

Above is an optional design that can be made by following instructions at right.

1. Top and background fabric shown is chiffon. For added stability when stitching, cotton fabric may be used as background fabric. Sew three sides of "pocket." Place embellishment between two fabric layers. Complete stitching.

2. Follow arrows and sew completely to opposite edge to form pockets. Stitch center lines first, working outward to avoid puckering. Stitch lines with the grain first and lines on the bias last.

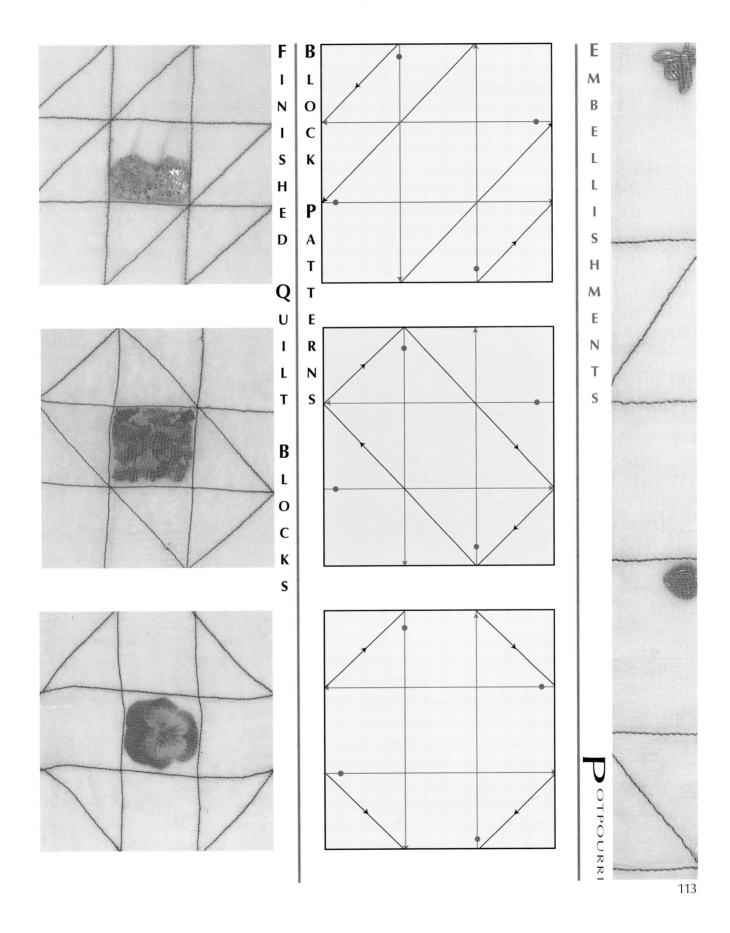

113

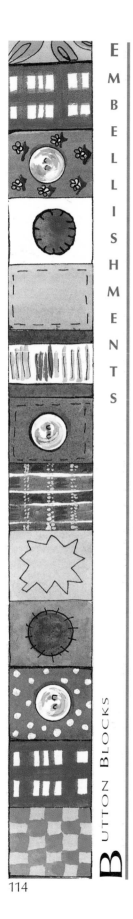

B UTTON BLOCKS

General: Appliqué in layers. Sew on buttons.

General: Draw details, using fabric pen.

General Option: Sew details with embroidery floss.

Specific Idea: Adhere decorative ribbon onto edges.

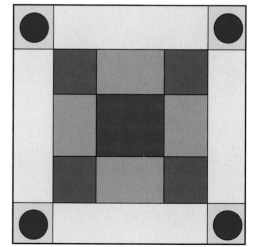

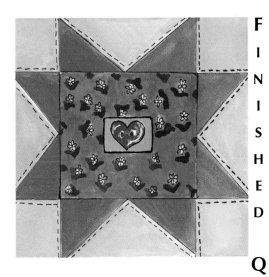

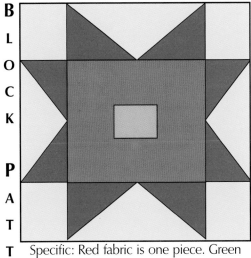

Specific: Red fabric is one piece. Green fabric is appliquéd over red fabric.

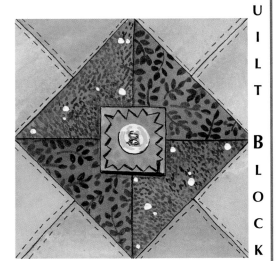

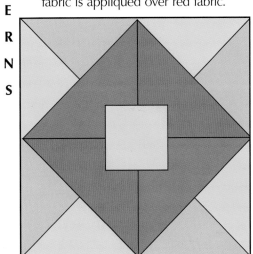

Specific: Yellow fabric is one piece. Green fabric is appliquéd over yellow fabric.

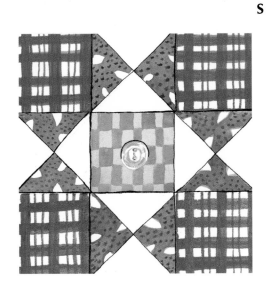

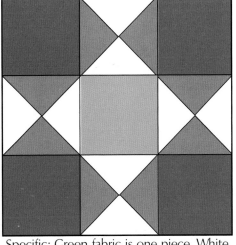

Specific: Green fabric is one piece. White fabric is appliquéd over yellow fabric.

BUTTON BLOCKS

General: Embellish with silk roses, beads,
and jute, etc.

General Option: Pad slightly with cotton
batting.

General: Turn heart pattern as indicated.

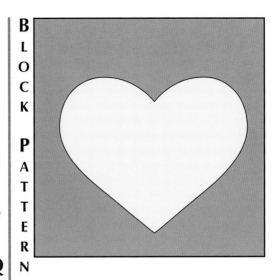

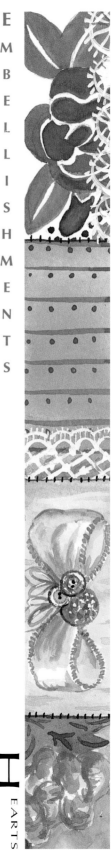

General: Add batting behind doily and adhere onto background fabric.

117

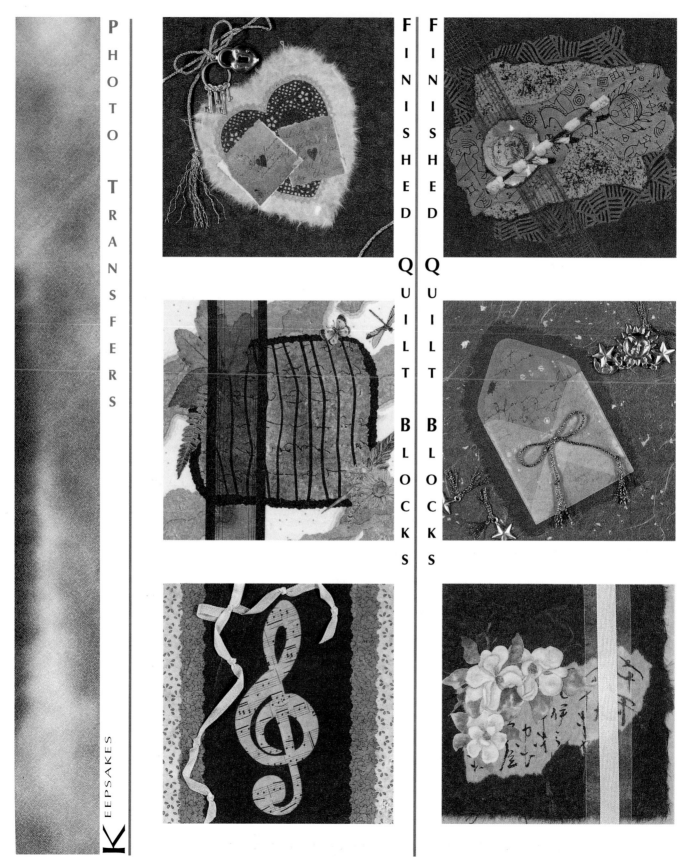

FINISHED QUILT BLOCKS

FINISHED QUILT BLOCKS

KEEPSAKES

Keepsakes

Materials & Tools

Cardstock: assorted colors, 8½" X 11"
Charms: brass, assorted
Fabric: cotton, white
Gift wrap: assorted with writing
Handmade papers: assorted colors
Iron/ironing board
Metallic braid: assorted
Old letters or post cards
Paper doilies: assorted
Photo tabs: ½" x ½"
Photo transfer paper: 8½" x 11"
Ribbon
Ruler
Scissors: craft; decorative–edged
Sewing needle
Sewing thread: coordinating color
Tissue paper: assorted, fancy

1. Organize all materials and tools needed for project.

2. Using craft scissors and ruler, cut cardstock in 8" x 8" squares.

3. Layout paper doilies, gift wrap, and papers. Layer until desired look is achieved.

4. Create decorative edging on gift wrap or paper, using decorative-edged scissors. Option: Using a small wet paintbrush, outline on gift wrap or paper where doilies, gift wrap, letters, papers will be. Tear carefully where water has been applied.

5. Attach layers to cardstock squares with photo tabs.

6. Take designed squares and photo transfer paper to a copy shop. Make a test copy on white copy paper, reducing 50% for a 4" x 4" quilt square. Explain to printer the exact look desired, including end size and reversed imaging for lettering. When desired effect is achieved, color–copy onto photo transfer paper. If using a photo transfer medium, color–copy onto white copy paper.

7. Place imaged side of transfer paper on white cotton fabric. Using a dry iron, press transfer paper onto fabric until image is successfully transferred to fabric, following manufacturer's instructions. Remove transfer paper. If using a photo transfer medium, transfer color–copy onto fabric, following manufacturer's instructions.

8. Sew assorted embellishments onto quilt squares, using needle with thread.

P H O T O   T R A N S F E R S

S CHOOL DAYS

F I N I S H E D   Q U I L T   B L O C K S

F I N I S H E D   Q U I L T   B L O C K S

Certificate of

PROMOTION

This certifies that

Devery Ferrin

successfully completed _Third Grade_
and is promoted to _Fourth Grade_

Presented at _Grandview Elementary School_
This _30th_ day of _May_ 1985

Signed _Mrs. Holm_

School Days

Materials & Tools

Craft scissors
Fabric: cotton, white, blue
Iron/ironing board
Paper: school theme or bright colors

Photo tabs: ½″ x ½″
Photo transfer paper: 8½″ x 11″
Ruler
School memorabilia: drawings, reports, report cards, etc.

1. Organize all materials and tools needed for project.

2. Take school memorabilia squares and photo transfer paper to a copy shop. Using a color copier, copy school memorabilia on white copy paper. Reduce certificates and large items for easy handling and placement.

3. Using craft scissors and ruler, cut background paper into desired quilt–square size.

4. Using craft scissors, cut around memorabilia. Attach memorabilia to background paper with photo tabs.

5. Make a test copy on white copy paper. Explain to printer the exact look desired, including end size and reversed imaging for lettering. When desired effect is achieved, color–copy onto photo transfer paper. If using a photo transfer medium, color–copy onto white copy paper.

6. Place imaged side of transfer paper on white cotton fabric. Using a dry iron, press transfer paper to fabric until image is successfully transferred to fabric, following manufacturer's instructions. Remove transfer paper. If using a photo transfer medium, transfer color copy onto fabric, following manufacturer's instructions.

General Option: Make a tree ornament for relatives with children's artwork.

General Option: Make a T-shirt of yearbook signatures.

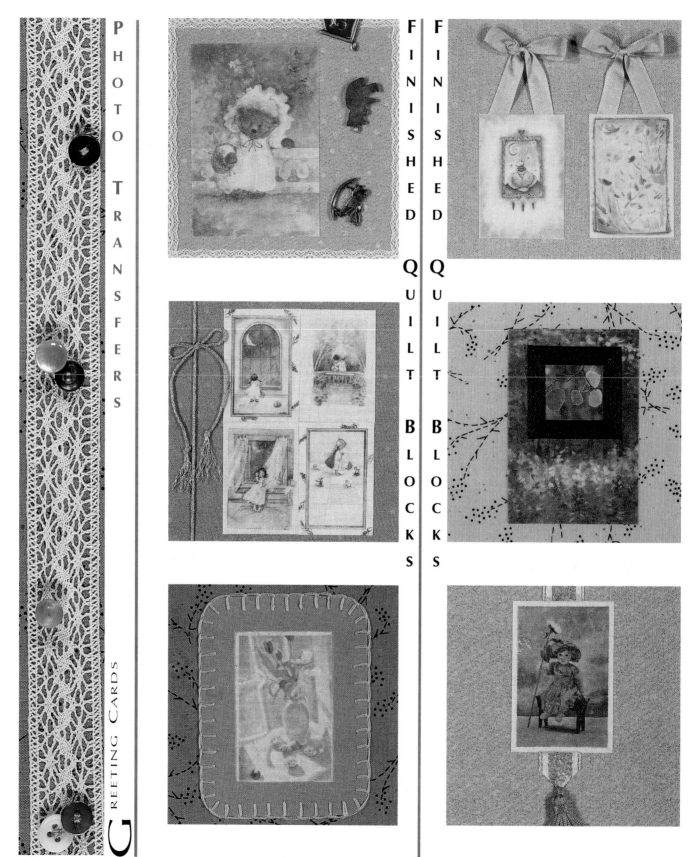

FINISHED QUILT BLOCKS

FINISHED QUILT BLOCKS

Greeting Cards

Materials & Tools

Embellishments: charms, and ribbons
Fabric: cotton, white for transfers;
    cotton, assorted for backgrounds
Fabric scissors
Fusible web

Greeting cards: assorted sizes
Iron/ironing board
Measuring tape or ruler
Photo transfer paper
Sewing needle
Sewing thread

1. Organize all materials and tools needed for project.

2. Take greeting cards and photo transfer paper to a copy shop. Make a test copy on white copy paper. Explain to printer the exact look desired, including end size and reversed imaging for lettering. When desired effect is achieved, color–copy onto photo transfer paper. If using a photo transfer medium, color–copy onto white copy paper.

3. Place imaged side of transfer paper on white cotton fabric. Using a dry iron, press transfer paper to fabric until image is successfully transferred to fabric, following manufacturer's instructions. Remove transfer paper. If using a photo transfer medium, transfer color copy onto fabric, following manufacturer's instructions.

4. Using fabric scissors, cut around transfers, leaving a ½" white border around edge.

5. Place a piece of discarded web backing between white cotton transfer and ironing board. Adhere wrong side of white cotton transfer to right side of background fabric with fusible web, following manufacturer's instructions.

6. Sew assorted embellishments onto quilt squares, using a needle with thread.

General Option: Make a pillow with a favorite card.

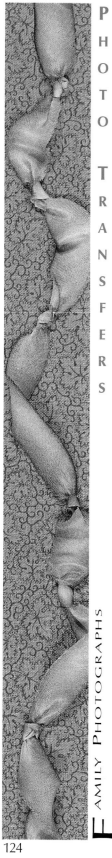

F
I
N
I
S
H
E
D

Q
U
I
L
T

B
L
O
C
K
S

F
I
N
I
S
H
E
D

Q
U
I
L
T

B
L
O
C
K
S

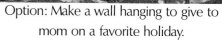

Option: Make a wall hanging to give to mom on a favorite holiday.

Family Photographs

Materials & Tools

Cardstock: assorted, 8½" x 11"
Catalogs, magazines
Craft scissors
Fabric: cotton, white

Family photographs
Iron/ironing
Photo tabs: ½" x ½"
Photo transfer paper: 8½" x 11"
Ruler

---

1. Organize all materials and tools needed for project.

2. Using craft scissors and ruler, cut cardstock into 8" x 8" squares.

3. Using color copier, copy family photographs, reducing to desired size.

4. Using craft scissors, cut around copied photographs and attach to cardstock squares with photo tabs.

5. Create a theme to go along with each photo square. Create decorative edging where desired with old catalog and magazine pictures relating to each theme. Attach pictures to cardstock squares with photo tabs.

6. Take theme squares and photo transfer paper to a copy shop. Make a test copy on white copy paper. Explain to printer the exact look desired, including end size and reversed imaging for lettering. When desired effect is achieved, color–copy onto photo transfer paper. If using a photo transfer medium, color–copy onto white copy paper.

7. Place imaged side of transfer paper on white cotton fabric. Using a dry iron, press transfer paper to fabric until image is successfully transferred to fabric, following manufacturer's instructions. Remove transfer paper. If using a photo transfer medium, transfer color copy onto fabric, following manufacturer's instructions.

General Option: Make a memory album of grandparents

General Option: Make a wall hanging to give to mom on a favorite holiday.

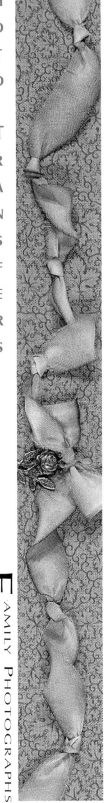

mm—Millimetres cm—Centimetres

Inches to Millimetres and Centimetres

inches	mm	cm	inches	cm	inches	cm
⅛	3	0.3	9	22.9	30	76.2
¼	6	0.6	10	25.4	31	78.7
½	13	1.3	12	30.5	33	83.8
⅝	16	1.6	13	33.0	34	86.4
¾	19	1.9	14	35.6	35	88.9
⅞	22	2.2	15	38.1	36	91.4
1	25	2.5	16	40.6	37	94.0
1¼	32	3.2	17	43.2	38	96.5
1½	38	3.8	18	45.7	39	99.1
1¾	44	4.4	19	48.3	40	101.6
2	51	5.1	20	50.8	41	104.1
2½	64	6.4	21	53.3	42	106.7
3	76	7.6	22	55.9	43	109.2
3½	89	8.9	23	58.4	44	111.8
4	102	10.2	24	61.0	45	114.3
4½	114	11.4	25	63.5	46	116.8
5	127	12.7	26	66.0	47	119.4
6	152	15.2	27	68.6	48	121.9
7	178	17.8	28	71.1	49	124.5
8	203	20.3	29	73.7	50	127.0

Contents 3